TYPOGRAPHICAL PERIODICALS
BETWEEN THE WARS

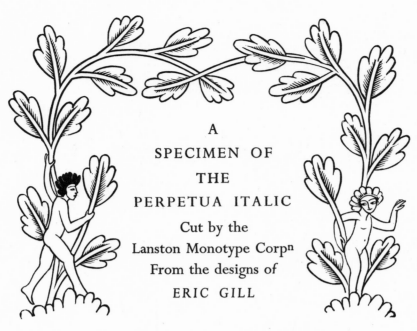

A
SPECIMEN OF
THE
PERPETUA ITALIC
Cut by the
Lanston Monotype Corp^n
From the designs of
ERIC GILL

This ken *we* truly, that as *wonder* to intellect,
so for the soul desire of beauty is mover and spring;
whence, in whatever his spirit is most moved, a man
wil most be engaged with beauty; and thus in his 'first love'
physical beauty and spiritual are both present
mingled inseparably in his lure: then is he seen
in the ecstasy of earthly passion and of heavenly vision
to fall to idolatry of some specious appearance
as if 'twer very incarnation of his heart's desire,
whether eternal and spiritual, as with Dante it was,
or mere sensuous perfection, or as most commonly
a fusion of both—when if distractedly he hav thought
to mate mortally with an eternal essence
all the delinquencies of his high passion ensue.

Fig. 10. *First proof of Perpetua italic (before changes in fitting)*

The Fleuron No. 7: 'First Proof of Perpetua Italic'.

Grant Shipcott

TYPOGRAPHICAL PERIODICALS BETWEEN THE WARS

A Critique of The Fleuron, Signature and Typography

1980

OXFORD POLYTECHNIC PRESS

Editors   Anne Rummey and Steve Thompson
Indexer   Janine Amos
Illustration research   Stella Paskins
Design   Viv Harper and James Maughan
Production   Ann Byrne, Viv Harper, Mary Hoare, Suzanne Luchford,
   Sarah Menon and Anne Rummey
Publicity and Sales   Karen Geddes, Jessica Kent and Linda Magnus-Andresen
© Grant Shipcott 1980
First published 1980 by Oxford Polytechnic Press, Headington, Oxford OX3 OBP
Set in 12 on 14 point Monotype Bembo
Printed by offset lithography on Basingwerk Parchment by Cotswold Press,
Ferry Hinksey Road, Oxford
Bound by Kemp Hall Bindery, Oxford
Hardback edition: 100 numbered copies ISBN 0 902692 19 4
Paperback edition: 400 numbered copies ISBN 0 902692 20 8

Shipcott, Grant
   Typographical periodicals between the wars.
   1. Fleuron, The
   2. Signature
   3. Typography
   I. Title
   686.2′2′05   Z119

   ISBN 0-902692-19-4
   ISBN 0-902692-20-8 Pbk

Preface

IN WRITING THE DISSERTATION which was the precursor to this book, I confined my researches to the Bodleian Library, Oxford, and to a series of prolonged and somewhat diverse conversations with my tutor, Tom Colverson, to whom I owe the greatest debt of thanks. For their help in the preparation of this rewritten version I must thank the following: Nicolas Barker, Basil Harley of the Curwen Press, Robert Harling, Ellic Howe, Ruari McLean, James Mosley and the Library at the St Bride's Institute, London, and Vivian Ridler, recently retired as Printer to Oxford University Press. Thanks also go to Robert Harling, the executors of the estate of Stanley Morison, and John Dreyfus, Typographic Adviser to the Printing Division at Cambridge University Press, for granting permission to reproduce illustrations and textual matter. I am particularly grateful to Vivian Ridler and his successor, Eric Buckley, for making available the facilities of Oxford University Press to provide the illustrations. We are proud to have the opportunity to work alongside the staff of the Press. I am also grateful to Fiona Bailey and Margaret O'Brien for typing the manuscript.

Oxford, October 1978   R.J.G.S.

Contents

Publisher's Note

ALL THREE PERIODICALS were published long before metrication was introduced in the United Kingdom. In order to avoid the confusion which might arise from giving metric measurements, we give in Appendix 1 all the original Imperial dimensions of each publication.

So far as is possible we reproduce subjects in the same size as used in the relevant periodical. Exceptions are: 10, 22, 23, 24, 27, 31, 32, 33, 35, 37, 38, 39, 40, 41, 42, 43, 44, 45, 46, 47, 48, 49 and 50 (slightly reduced); 4a, 4b, 4c, 8 and 29 (substantially reduced).

All illustrations are here reproduced in either one or two colours – black or black and red. The second colour, red, is used only where the original reproduction was printed in either black and red (3, 6, 7, 9, 10, 12, 15, 16, 17, 18, 19, 23, 36) or black and blue (38).

There are two subjects originally reproduced in three colours – black, blue and red – and these have, for reasons of convenience and economy, been converted to black and white (13 and 45).

Illustrations

Foreword

ANYONE IS LIKELY TO BE SURPRISED to find that an enterprise engaged upon light-heartedly when young had now become the object of earnest academic enquiry.

Such was my reaction to Grant Shipcott's dissertation. The typescript arrived, franked with the post-mark 'Oxford', but needing a latterday Einstein to define its true relativity in time and space. The story evoked a personal world light-years removed from the present scene.

Almost all the main characters involved in the story are now dead. Only Ellic Howe and myself are still (very much) alive. This felicitous condition (for us) is doubtless due to the fact that we were both a good deal younger – and probably more light-hearted – than the other characters involved.

To me, Grant Shipcott's tale reads true to life. Above all, his narration underlines one formidable difference between then and now. Young men have always wanted to rush into print: young designers as keenly as young writers. In those days, such headstrong characters could publish their manifestos on fairly reasonable terms. When James Shand, Ellic Howe and myself first discussed the possibility of publishing *Typography*, we weren't especially daunted by the probable costs involved. Admittedly, Howe was well-heeled, Shand was the son of a successful printer and I was agreeably and gainfully employed as a designer, but cost was not our main concern. We knew we should be able to achieve what we were after within our budget.

Not so today. Young men wishful to make a similar bid to give their notions graphic shape are immediately intimidated by the likely cost. At best they have to go looking for sponsors: at worst they have to call the whole thing off.

Quite recently, in discussions with Rowley Atterbury and Eva Svensson of the Westerham Press concerning the possibility of reviving *Alphabet and Image* (the post-war successor to the *Typography* of Grant Shipcott's story), I was appalled by the costs involved – and those from a printer keen to press on and make things easy! Far cry from the background to the journals documented in these pages.

Morison and Simon started *The Fleuron*, probably the most influential printing journal ever to be published in the Western World, on a hopeful shoestring; *Signature* and *Typography* were readily subsidised by their eager founders and committed printers and sympathetically supported by indulgent advertisers: process-engravers, paper-makers, publishers and so on. But where are such printers and patrons in today's economic climate of printing conglomerates and computerised setting? A long long way off.

Which is sad, for the printing industry, now in such a traumatic technological transition, needs such journals, edited and written by outsiders looking in. Printing has always suspiciously encouraged – and profited from – the enquiries of the enthusiastic amateur.

And young men themselves need the lively mental stimulus occasioned by such activities, whether as participants or students. For me, collecting Volume VII of *The Fleuron* from Zwemmer's bookshop in the Charing Cross Road was as heady an aesthetic experience as my first sight of Venice. For others, too. That notable wood engraver, Reynolds Stone, told me last year of a similar experience. Entering the Cambridge University Press as a trainee from the University, he discovered that one of the printers there, by the memorable name of Mr Nobbs, had a complete set of *The Fleuron*. That journal of typography changed Stone's life, as it changed mine.

Congratulations, then, to Grant Shipcott, for putting down these records of the activities of a group of men from an earlier generation, all of whom were wholly hooked on printing and its manifold enchantments.

ROBERT HARLING

TYPOGRAPHICAL PERIODICALS BETWEEN THE WARS

Typography.

II.

WHAT TYPE IS.

HOW IT IS MANUFACTURED.

YPES, declares the author of the "Mirrour of Pryntyng," "to they that be of the Craft are as things that be alive. He is an ill Worker that handleth them not gently and with Reverence. In them is the power of Thought contained, and all that cometh therefrom."

We have no quarrel with that sentiment, but we have here rather to deal with physical considerations. As usually cast, a type has attached to it a "tang" or gate, which carries with it a small plug, generally a frustrum of a cone. This is known as the dot; and this dot consists of metal which was contained in a piece intermediate between the mould and the nozzle of the metal pot, from which the supply of liquid metal for casting the type is ejected. The tang of course has to be removed, and the lower surface or foot of the type must be dressed or grooved so as to get rid of the projecting irregularities resulting from fracture of. the tang. This operation has usually been carried out by hand, and the types, after the removal of the tang, are then set up also by hand on sticks preparatory to their transfer to the dressing bench. Here the irregularities at the break are removed by the passage of a hand-plane along the inverted line of type, the plane at the same time producing what is known as the foot or heel-nick. Hitherto this groove has been considered as essential to good type; but the modern practice, supported by the experience gained from several machines which cast and trim the type by other methods, or cast the type perfect in respect to its foot bearing, has shown that the mere removal of any projecting metal is all that is really necessary, and that the provision of the heel-nick as a distinct depression is quite unnecessary.

NOMENCLATURE OF TYPE.

The names for the various parts of a type will be seen by reference to Figure 1.

The names of the various parts of the face of a type and of its dimensions may be seen by reference to Figures 1 and 2.

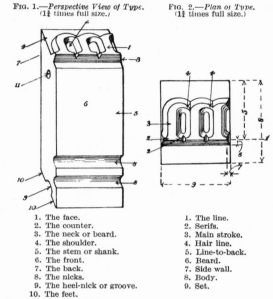

FIG. 1.—*Perspective View of Type.*
(1¼ times full size.)

FIG. 2.—*Plan of Type.*
(1¼ times full size.)

1. The face.
2. The counter.
3. The neck or beard.
4. The shoulder.
5. The stem or shank.
6. The front.
7. The back.
8. The nicks.
9. The heel-nick or groove.
10. The feet.
11. The pin-mark.

1. The line.
2. Serifs.
3. Main stroke.
4. Hair line.
5. Line-to-back.
6. Beard.
7. Side wall.
8. Body.
9. Set.

The dimension given above as side wall does not appear to have had a name until recently, when it was called thus in the matrices of the Wicks typecasting machine.

The distance from the face to the shoulder is known as the depth of strike.

In addition to the names given to the various parts shown in Figures 1 and 2, certain portions of characters have names of their own; for example, the round portion of the b d p q surrounding the counter is known as the "bowl," the bulb at the end of the tail of the f j y is the "tail-dot," the lugs at the top of the capital C and G are sometimes called "cat's ears," and the sharp extremities of the counters of the M N V W and of many other characters are styled "crotches."

Various devices, which, however, at present are by no means universally employed, have

Introduction

In THE QUARTER-CENTURY before the First World War the concepts of book design and production changed drastically and irreversibly. The changes were brought about by personalities, by technological changes and by economic necessity. The technological advances at this time were many, but the most important were the much-needed invention of mechanical type-setters, and process engraving. Mechanical type-setters were necessary not only to save labour but also to contain the boom in the printing industry caused largely by the increase in education. The invention of photography and the half-tone process greatly expanded the possibilities of illustration; in 1889 *Penrose's Annual* claimed that the half-tone process 'can't get any better', though in the light of subsequent developments, especially paper manufacture, that statement should be qualified somewhat.

The most far-reaching changes were brought about by individual achievement. The most outstanding figures in printing at this time were those involved with the private presses. When discussing the private press movement, one must remember that William Morris and his contemporaries rejected mechanical processes, be it on aesthetic or socialist (employment) grounds. Private press publications are more often reminiscent of sixteenth-century printing than of Victorian printing. Morris wrote: 'I began printing books with the hope of producing some which would have a definite claim to beauty, while at the same time they should be easy to read and should not dazzle the eye, or trouble the intellect of the reader by eccentricity of form in the letters.'[1] The Kelmscott Press books are certainly beautiful, but the Golden and Chaucer types are not the most legible of faces. Morris's priorities were questionable from the start; in the same note he writes: 'It was a matter of course that I should consider it necessary that the paper should be hand-made, both for the sake of durability and appearance. It would be very false economy to stint in the quality of paper as to price: so I had only to think about the kind of hand-made paper.'[2] The use of hand-made paper together with hand-set proprietary founders' types, hand-printed and hand-bound, made these books highly expensive and thus

1. *The Times Printing Number:* 'Typography II – What Type Is'.

available only to the rich. If the prime function of a book is communication (and printed books should by definition provide mass communication) then Morris failed as a publisher; but he was chiefly concerned with showing to those who cared that beauty can be an integral part of a printed book. For that ideal his work must be acclaimed as one of the most beneficial influences on twentieth-century printing. Controversy over the way in which he implemented that ideal carried on for several decades.

Another man who made a profound impression on the publishing and printing trades before the First World War was Joseph Malaby Dent. An admirer of Morris, he was struck by the idea of starting a series of volumes of world literature at 'the democratic price of one shilling' that would appeal to 'the worker, the student, the cultured man, the child, the man and woman'. Dent undertook to issue one thousand books over several years, fifty at a time, and one hundred and fifty in the first twelve months. As he recalled: 'We had to print at least ten thousand of each volume to cover the bare cost, and in many cases – notably of Shakespeare and Dickens – as many as twenty or thirty thousand. For my fixed determination was to make it a democratic library at the democratic price of one shilling.'[3] The scheme met with instant and deserved success, so much so that most of the profit had to be invested in reprints. The books were printed on strong, thin but opaque paper, making each volume a genuine pocket book. The design of the title pages and end-papers was very similar to that of some Kelmscott Press books, with complex flowered borders and Renaissance-influenced typography. The text, however, has hardly dated to the present day, save for the large spaces after each full point. Dent's Everyman's Library was a real step into the twentieth century, though some book lovers were inclined to see it as a retrogressive step.

If a bibliophile wanted to find out for himself about these and other changes in the trade, he was obliged to plough through such periodicals as *The British Printer*, *The British and Colonial Printer* or *Penrose's Annual*. If he could understand all the technicalities he still had to see past the editor's loyalties and wade through pages of advertisements. This 'closed shop' aura surrounding the printing world was remedied on 10 September 1912 with the appearance of *The Times Printing Number* to mark the 40,000th issue of that newspaper. Although not strictly a periodical, the *Number* merits a brief examination for several reasons. In its time it was the only (single volume) source which contained the most up-to-date information on printing, the list of contents including 'Typography', 'Printing Machinery', 'Colour Printing', 'Papermaking', 'Ink', 'Bookbinding', 'Modern Methods and Machinery', and articles on modern printing in Germany and the USA. On that account, it is still a most useful textbook for the student of printing. Even if it were not remarkable in that way it would still be mentioned here for two other reasons. Firstly it was *The Times Printing Number* that persuaded a young bank clerk named Stanley Morison to make a career for himself in the printing industry. Secondly it

2. *The Imprint* No. 5: 'Decoration and its Uses V – The Choice of Letter Forms and the Simple Arrangement of Letters' by Edward Johnston.

types—though they seem nearly to fill the whole field of vision—are themselves a variety (or varieties). I give here (fig. 21) a reasonably

ABCDEFGHIJKLMNOPQRSTUVWXYZ Skeltns.

PEN:ABCDHIJMOR

abcdefghijklmnopqrstuvwxyz "roman" small-letter Skeletons.

pen-abcdfghijklmoqrstuv

xyz "rom". foundational han

abcdefghijklmnopqrstuvwxyz italic skeletons

pen-abcdefghijklmoqrstuvwxyz

Fig. 21. Skeletons of the current standard forms and a suggested Pen standard (in oblique-nib writing). Note : The natural pen hooks and strokes are here used for terminals or serifs.

representative version of this pen standard. The pen standard, which with a little care we can all of us recreate, has the peculiar virtue—as far as the small-letters are concerned—of being essentially the ancestral type (so that, literally, all other varieties are varieties of it). The example of it is given here in the hope that decorators may acquire it, or a similar formal hand. Having such hands at our command, we may experiment freely in form and arrangement of letters, and it is certain that most of us can in this way discover the " theory and practice " of decoration more easily and surely than by any other means.

Simple written Roman Capitals. It will be remembered that certain early

was in *The Times Printing Number* that *The Imprint* ('an illustrated monthly magazine price 1/- net, devoted to the printing and allied trades') was first advertised, listing its editors, advisers and aims, though there was no mention of the new Imprint typeface, which was to be introduced for the first time in that periodical.

The interest in printing created by *The Times Printing Number* paved the way for the success of *The Imprint*, the first number of which appeared in January 1913. It set the tone and style for the typographical periodicals of later years: sober, well-reasoned articles by distinguished contributors, lush illustration printed by various processes and strong emphasis on correspondence. The editors expressed their views and aims in the first number:

> We see around us high technical skill, but almost no culture or taste. The artistic possibilities of lithography are scarcely realised by the public or the trade. In letterpress printing, men cling to a tradition in its degenerate forms – when they should reach back to the finer work of an earlier birth: or, again, they waste themselves in mere ingenuity and artifice, or strive to appear something that they are not – try to rival the lithographer in colour, or the copperplate engraver in freedom and fineness of line.
>
> The Kelmscott Press, the Doves Press, and the Ashendene Press have done a great deal towards bringing about a Renaissance of Printing, and though the commercial printer is prone to speak slightingly of the private presses, much of the improvement in his own work, especially in the design of the types he uses, is to be derived from this source.[4]

The editors of *The Imprint* made their own contribution to type design by designing and having Monotype cut a new face specially for the periodical. The design was based on Caslon and Plantin Old Faces, with modern printing conditions in mind. Imprint Old Face (Series 101), the first general printing face to be made universally available for fifty years, is still used for many printing jobs today. It is to the editors' credit that no attempt was made to reserve Imprint to the periodical: 'Our policy is sincerely to improve the craft of which we are so proud.'[5]

Unfortunately, and for no apparent reason, *The Imprint* was discontinued early in 1914. (L. T. Owens suggests that the demise of *The Imprint* was due to disagreements between the contributors and the publisher, Gerard Meynell.[6]) It helped to widen interest in the graphic arts with a new scholarly approach to the subject; its edition of 10,000 shows how widespread the interest had become. Ten years later, after the enormous changes in society and attitudes brought about by the First World War, a superior imitation of *The Imprint*, edited by two of the foremost typographers of this century, was to appear under the name *The Fleuron*.

3. *The Imprint* No. 8: 'Notes on Some Liturgical Books' by Stanley Morison.

Fig. 6—Page from Sarum Missal, 1494, showing portion of marriage service.

The Marriage service is occasionally found bound up with the Missal. Fig. 6 is from the Sarum Missal of Frederick Egmont, and shows a part of the Marriage service, in which the printer, being a foreigner, has left space for the vernacular portion to be added by hand. The MS. notes read as follows :—

I, N, take the N to my weddide housbōde, to have and to holde, for bett^r for wars, for richer for porer, ī siknes and ī helth, to be honored and loved at bed and at bord, tyll deth us depart if holy chirche will it orden, and therto I plyghte the my trouthe.

W^t this rynge I the wed, and this golde and silver I the gife, and with my body I the wership and w^t all my worldly catell ye endow.

Fig. 1.—*Cancelleresca formata* from Ferdinando Ruano: *Sette Alfabeti*, Rome, 1554

Frate vespasiano Amphyarw.

L a grandissima beneuolentia, qual porto al nostro commune amico, Giouan bat
Ciardi. & Christofano amantissimo, mi ba constretto di mutar proposito, impero
chi sendomi quasi che deliberato di non uolere intagliare nell opra mia altra sor
te di scritur che quella Bastarda tanto fauorita, pure sapendo poi quanta indi
natione egli alla mia Cancellarescv della quale tanto sollecitaua gli amati
figliuolini, in sua gratificatione le presenti pollice sono date in luce, ne altro occorch
se non che a V. S0. et albumanissimo cortesia sua infinitamente mi R accom.

Al suo Giouan Bamsta aardi.

Fig. 2.—An early *cancelleresca bastarda* (only slightly sloped and untied) from Vespasiano
Amphiareo: *Opera nella quale sinsegna a scriuere*, Venice, 1554

of the fine professional scribes. Though most of these professionals claimed to work by geometrical rules deduced from the classical inscriptions, Ferdinando Ruano, writer at the Vatican, is the only one who has left us a book giving the geometrical rules for the formation of minuscular *lettera cancelleresca*. There was also a comparatively informal hand of this kind and in several varieties, of which one or two duly appeared in type. Thus we find the Aldine italic cut by Francesco Griffo, of Venice, in 1500, and the italic cut by Ludovico Vicentino and Bartolomeo Lautizio, of Rome, in 1522. If we compare these we shall notice several important differences. The Aldine is a smaller letter, round and composed with many ligatures (the *Virgil* of 1501 possesses about sixty-five tied letters), by means of which the typefounder more successfully reproduced the script of his time. Composition with this elaborate series of characters was such that we are not surprised to find that later Aldine books used a smaller number of ligatures, and that other Italian printers who copied the type refrained from cutting more than a few characters of this kind. For Aldus the experiment was a serious one. He felt he had to produce as nearly good a reproduction as possible of the hand employed for current purposes. This hand was, as we have already stated, a variety of the *lettera cancelleresca*. It is strongly cursive in character, that is to say it is a running hand, in which the letters are tied more frequently than not. Obviously it is a hand developed by and for rapid writing. The type of Vicentino, 1522, is a larger, more considered and pointed design immediately based upon a pure form of the *cancelleresca*.

If the types be placed side by side, it is impossible not to conclude that the Aldine letter is inferior in design to that of Vicentino, and that the reason lies in the fact that, whereas the Venetian italic was based upon a comparatively hurried script, the Roman owes its form to a particularly pure and painstaking hand. The truth is, that though the italic of Aldus is first in order of time, in order of merit it must yield place to that of Vicentino. In other words, the less perfect Venetian form appears in type twenty years in advance of the perfect Roman form.

The finest practitioners of the *cancelleresca* were to be found in Rome and Florence rather than in Venice. Nevertheless, as, in any case, it was the ambition of Aldus to issue cheap handy texts of the classics, the letter of his choice was justified at least by reason of its greater economy in space consumption than that of the more elegant Roman forms.

It was the evident purpose of Vicentino, on the other hand, to issue works

---

AN INTRODUCTION
TO HEBREW TYPOGRAPHY

By

ELLIC HOWE

ITALY, 1475–1600

Hebrew printing has its Coster. In the *Zeitschrift fuer Hebraeische Bibliographie* (8 : 46) it has been suggested that Hebrew matrices were in the possession of a Jew in Avignon as early as 1444. But the claims of Davin, of Caderousse, are not very well substantiated. It is generally accepted that the first product of the Hebrew press was *A Commentary on the Pentateuch*, printed in Reggio di Calabria by Abraham ben Garton in 1475. In the same year the physician Meshullam printed the great code of law, *The Four Pillars*, at Pieve di Sacco, an obscure hamlet in the Venetian Lagoon. Within the next few years we hear of isolated activities on the part of a few Hebrew presses: those of Abraham Conat at Mantua, Abraham the Dyer at Ferrara, Abraham Caravita at Bologna. But the work of these pioneers was overshadowed by that of Israel Soncino and his family, who produced four generations of printers between 1483 and 1547.

In 1478 Israel Soncino, whose father Samuel originated from Speyer in Alsace, was in business as a banker in the town of Soncino, from which he took his name. The founding of a municipal public loan office drove him out of business, and he turned his attention to the art of printing. His sons and grandsons assisted in the work. Their early productions were notable, including the *Mahzor*, or ritual for the year, the *Bible*, printed with the help of

12

אמר ר׳ יצחק לא ח״ח צריך לחתחי״ל
את התורה אלא מהחדש חוה לכם
שחיא מצוה ראשונה שוצטוו ישראל
ומה טעם פתח בבראשית משום כח

Type used for the first book printed in Hebrew. (*A Commentary on the Pentateuch.*) Reggio di Calabria, 1475

וכפתור תחת שני הקנים ממנה וכפתור
תחת שני הקנים ממנה וכפתור תחת
שני הקנים ממנה לששת הקנים היצ
האים מן המנרה: כפתריהם וקנתם
ממנה יהיו כלה מקשה אחת זהב
טהור: ועשית את נרתיה שבעה והעלה
את נרתיה והאיר על עבר פניה:

Type of Gerson Soncino, cut circa 1491

אילו

דברים שאוכל להם שיעור הפארה והבכורים
והראיון וגמילות חסדים ותלמוד תורה ״אילו
דברים שאדם אוכל פירותיהן בעולם הזה
והקרן קיימת לו לעולם הבא כבוד אב ואם
וגמילות חסד והבאת שלום בין אדם לחבירו
ותלמוד תורה כנגד כולם ׃ אין

Type of Daniel Bomberg, Venice, cut circa 1540

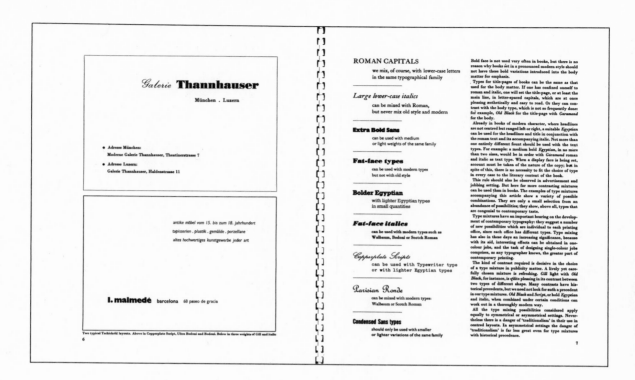

The greatly reduced illustrations on this opening show the comparative shapes and sizes of spreads of The Fleuron, Signature *and* Typography.
The original page sizes are:
The Fleuron: 11⅛ ins. × 8¾ ins.; Signature: 9¾ins. × 7⅜ ins.;
Typography: 11 ins. × 9 ins.

I

The Fleuron

THE STORY BEHIND THE CONCEPTION of *The Fleuron* is best recounted in Oliver Simon's autobiography *Printer and Playground*, and I have précised Simon here in order to understand the views of that periodical especially with regard to machine printing. Late in 1921, only two years after Simon had first become interested in printing, he accompanied Harold Curwen to a meeting convened to discuss 'publicity for the advancement of the cause of good printing'; at that meeting, Simon and Stanley Morison met for the first time. A year later they met again together with Francis Meynell, Holbrook Jackson and Bernard Newdigate, with the intention of setting up a publishing society primarily concerned with demonstrating that machine-set and machine-printed books could be as beautiful as those produced so laboriously by the private presses. The name of The Fleuron Society, suggested by Meynell, was agreed upon. At the next meeting the society disbanded, mainly because Newdigate still upheld his view of the superiority of hand-printing. Francis Meynell enlarges on that situation in his autobiography:

> I gave the society its name, but did I contribute to the 'storms' [Simon's word]? As I remember the meetings, a truer word would have been 'differences': Newdigate wanted to retain hand-setting and hand-made papers and specialize in narrowly limited editions; Holbrook Jackson wanted no limits at all; Oliver was, I think, depressed by the number of strongly opinionated people who had come together (he could never adjust to a committee of more than one); I wanted to combine mechanical production with larger limits to editions.[1]

Simon's own attitude towards hand-production must be examined, as it shows great advancement upon that of *The Imprint*:

> ... the influence of the Private Press movement had passed its peak at the time of the Fleuron Society and critics were appearing who questioned its practice and

5. *The Fleuron* No. 1: 'Initial Letters in the Printed Book' by Percy Smith.

direction. I found myself undergoing a gradual change of outlook . . . My admiration . . . for the personalities and integrity of Emery Walker and St John Hornby . . . remained high, but I could not admit that it was desirable to work in an idiom of an age long past, in their case mainly Italian Renaissance. Many of their books, forced into a Renaissance mould, had an air of unreality about them. It seemed to me that the economic and social conditions of our own time, and the use of modern machinery supporting imagination and intelligence, would, as in all good periods of printing, inevitably yet gradually be contributory factors in remoulding typographic style.[2]

The editors of *The Imprint* were understandably very much in awe of the achievements of the private presses; in the initial blaze of superior quality, it was easy to reject any objections to such a minor factor as archaism. In the 'modern' and newly optimistic twenties, men like Simon and Meynell were able to make more objective and critical judgements on what was once almost a sacred subject. It was time for everyone to accept that the machine age had truly and permanently arrived.

After the abortive second meeting of the Fleuron Society, Simon and Morison stayed together and quickly came to the conclusion that they should start a typographical periodical. Simon suggested that it should be named 'Typographical Journal'; Morison thought that too stiff and suggested 'The Fleuron'. They canvassed the other Fleuron Society members for contributions as well as several trade colleagues, and prepared to publish the first number early in 1923.

The two men were almost ideally qualified for the task they had set themselves. They were both young, with a flair for their chosen profession, taking real pleasure in imparting knowledge to others. Compared with some of their contemporaries, particularly the Continentals, they could not be said to be radical or controversial (typographically speaking), but their opinions were always worthwhile, never trivial or outrageous. One might rightly accuse them, especially Morison, of conservatism; not only did they want printing to stay much as it was in 1923, but they did not hesitate to reach back into the past to 'borrow' what seemed relevant to the modern age. As James Moran points out,[3] a study of *The Fleuron* reveals that the core of contributors were also taking most of the typographical initiative at the time; this was particularly true of Stanley Morison, who as typographical adviser to the Monotype Corporation and later to Cambridge University Press exerted a very great influence. Under his direction, the classic faces of the past, Baskerville, Bembo, Garamond and Walbaum among them, were modified and made available for machine composition. Morison's production programme placed the Monotype Corporation in a position of eminence unique and unsurpassed in world printing.

Morison had just left the Cloister Press and Simon persuaded Harold Curwen to

6. *The Fleuron* No. 1: 'Emil Rudolf Weiss' by Julius Meier-Graefe. Title page, R. Piper und Co., Munich.

DRUCKE

DER MARÉES GESELLSCHAFT

herausgeber: J. MEIER-GRÆFE

DRITTE REIHE

Leitung: Dresden, Kaitzerstr. 4. Geschäfts
stelle: R. PIPER und Co: MÜNCHEN

acquire the old Cloister office in Westminster. St Stephen's House, or rather 'the Office of The Fleuron', served a number of purposes. Simon used it as a West End office of Curwen from which he carried out his function of selling print to book publishers, and it was a base from which to carry out his activities under the Fleuron imprint. Morison too used it as a London headquarters, although at this time he was as likely to be in Paris, Berlin, Lyon or Rome as in London, talking to printers, typographers or typefounders, or researching in libraries. Early in 1924, the office was moved to Great Russell Street in Bloomsbury, and it became a lively meeting place for friends and colleagues alike. Simon recalls the time fondly: 'For nearly three years I was at a sort of private University of Printing, where the company of Morison, the nature of our work and the variety of interesting visitors with their wit and contribution to discussion, moulded the lines which my career as a printer and editor were to take. . .'[4]

The articles for the seven issues were all obtained through personal contact. Many of the early contributors to *The Fleuron* were closely connected with Oliver Simon – Percy Smith did much work for Curwen; William Rothenstein was Simon's uncle; Hubert Foss was a close friend. Morison worked hard to get many of the later articles written: D. B. Updike at first refused but Morison eventually talked him round; his correspondence with van Krimpen began in 1926, but 'Typography in Holland' and Jan van Krimpen's binding designs did not appear until 1930; Eric Gill steadfastly refused to write anything, saying 'Typography is not my country', although he provided an engraving as the tailpiece for No. 7.

The fact that most of the prominent printers and printing scholars contributed to *The Fleuron* meant that a certain amount of self-approbation was inevitable. The first number includes a review of the twenty-fifth *Penrose's Annual*, and the author enthusiastically declares:

It has been stirred, as if by the kiss of fine typography, to a consciousness of the position it holds; it has awakened into eminence, beauty and character . . . Of perhaps more general interest is an article by Mr Stanley Morison on 'Printing in France, with especial interest to the Imprimerie Royale . . .'

That particular volume of *Penrose's Annual* was designed by Morison.

By publication day, a traveller, equipped with a four-page prospectus, had sold 103 copies of *The Fleuron* No. 1. In the prospectus Simon had asserted:

The principles which *The Fleuron* endeavours to promote by argument, it attempts to demonstrate by example; it is not confined within the rigid limits of commercialism. It is not merely as good as the price will permit, but as beautiful as a book can be, or if that be too high a claim, as good as its artists and workers can make it.[5]

7. *The Fleuron* No. 2: 'Mr C. H. St John Hornby's Ashendene Press' by Bernard Newdigate.

IT WAS IN SEPTEMBER, IN A TINY SUS-sex town which I had not quitted since the out-break of the war, & where the advent of our first handful of fugitives before the warning of Louvain & Aerschott & Termonde & Dinant had just been announced. Our small hill-top city, covering the steep sides of the compact pedestal crowned by its great church, had reserved a refuge at its highest point; and we had waited all day, from occasional train to train, for the moment at which we would attest our hospi-tality. It came at last, but late in the evening, when a vague outside rumour called me to my doorstep, where the unforgettable impres-sion at once assaulted me. Up the precipitous little street that led from the station, over the old grass-grown cobbles where vehicles rarely pass, came the panting procession of the homeless and their comforting, almost clinging entertainers, who seemed to hurry them on as in a sort of overflow of expression of the fever of charity. It was swift & eager, in the autumn darkness and under the flare of a single lamp—with no vociferation and, but for a woman's voice, scarce a sound save the shuffle of mounting feet & the thick-drawn breath of emotion. The note I except, however, was that of a young mother carrying her small child & surrounded by those who bore her on and on, almost lifting her as they went together. The reson-ance through our immemorial old street of her sobbing & sobbing cry was the voice itself of history; it brought home to me more things than I could then quite take the measure of, and these just because it expressed for her not direct anguish, but the incredibi-lity, as who should say, of honest assured protection. Months have elapsed, and from having been then one of a few hundred she is now one of scores & scores of thousands: yet her cry is still in my ears, whether to speak most of what she had lately or of what she actually felt; and it plays, to my own sense, as a great fitful, tragic light over the dark exposure of her people.

The first issue, and those that followed, certainly lived up to that assertion – the beauty and technical excellence of the production cannot fail to impress the modern observer, although it was received with no less admiration in 1923 than it is today. Bernard Newdigate, in the *London Mercury*, wrote: 'The first number of the *Fleuron* is a brilliant piece of book-production', and the reviewer in the *Manchester Guardian* wrote: 'Irreproachable in manner and execution . . . unlike some books on the subject, a notable example of the art it treats of.' J. C. Squire, writing in the *Observer*, wrote at some length on the healthy trends in the printing trade that he saw as being epitomised by *The Fleuron*:

Everybody interested in book production should secure this journal, which carries on, still more sumptuously, the work which was done before the war (1913) by the *Imprint*. It is the fruit of co-operation between a number of enthusiasts who are not private printers ministering to the tastes of connoisseurs with glass-fronted book-cases and large bank balances, but commercial printers willing to expend all this art on any job which is given to them – book, poster or prospectus. Every year adds to the number of commercial printing firms which are intelligently run by masters who realize how interesting this work is and by men who are taking an intelligent interest in what they do. Old firms are being regenerated, new ones are coming to birth; before long every big house will be compelled, one hopes, to adapt itself or go bankrupt.

Herbert Simon, in *Song and Words*, endorses this view:

The Fleuron was a declaration of faith in the new approach to printing; it was a new world in which competitors were welcomed as fellow warriors, and where there was rivalry it was rivalry of how best to forward the new outlook in printing . . . It was eloquent of the prevailing geniality that a young editor, then almost unknown, was able to get such wholesale support.[6]

The editor of the first four numbers was Oliver Simon; in the first number he acknowledges his 'indebtedness to Mr Stanley Morison for his constant advice and help in the production of this journal, and to Mr Harold Curwen for the many facilities given . . .'

Though these and other reviews were unanimously appreciative of the press-work there was a noticeable lack of enthusiasm for the content of No. 1. All five members of the Fleuron Society contributed, as well as William Rothenstein, Percy Smith and D. B. Updike. Morison and Francis Meynell collaborated on the opening article, 'Printers' Flowers and Arabesques', while Simon wrote a short but illuminating piece on 'The Title Page'. Though these and other articles were good, there was not sufficient drive to give *The Fleuron* the pioneering aura that it later

THE METROPOLITAN MUSEUM OF ART

CATALOGUE
OF A
MEMORIAL EXHIBITION
OF THE WORKS
OF
AUGUSTUS SAINT-GAUDENS

NEW YORK : MDCCCCVIII

CATALOGUE   31

*that in turn upon a mass of ribbon-bound laurel
supported upon a rectangular slab.*
Inscription
WILLIAM TECUMSEH SHERMAN.
Signature
AVGVSTVS SAINT-GAVDENS.
Lent by Mrs. Paul Thorndike.
NOTE. *Modeled from life in eighteen sittings. Served
as the study for the head of Sherman in the memorial
statue unveiled in 1903.*

57
MRS. SCHUYLER VAN RENSSE-
LAER
*Bronze plaque, low relief, signed and dated 1888.
H. 29¼ in.; W. 7¾ in. Head and shoulders,
side view, head profile, directed to the left.*
Inscription
ANIMVS NON OPVS. MDCCCLXXXVIII. TO
MARIANA GRISWOLD VAN RENSSELAER.
Signature
AVGVSTVS SAINT-GAVDENS.
Lent by Mrs. Schuyler Van Rensselaer.
NOTE. *A reduction is in the Luxembourg.*

58
JULES BASTIEN-LEPAGE
*Bronze plaque, low relief, signed and dated Paris,
1889. H. 14½ in.; W. 19½ in. Half length,*

8. *The Fleuron* No. 3:
'D. B. Updike and the
Merrymount Press'
by W. A. Dwiggins.
Printed by collotype.

embodied. Probably the most interesting article was written by Bernard Newdigate, 'Respice and Prospice', subtitled 'A Chronicle and a Forecast', which took a brief and general look at the past and future of printing. The man whose steadfast belief in hand-printing brought about the end of the Fleuron Society here encouraged further experiment in colour photolitho-offset and, under the heading 'The Doom of Typesetting', foresaw the advent of photosetting, though he offered no judgement on the merit of this possibility.

No. 2 was a marked improvement on its predecessor, particularly on account of articles by Updike and Morison. Updike, the director of the Merrymount Press, wrote, in 'On the Planning of Printing', that:

> . . . the best rules for planning work are general rules, and rules for the mind rather than for the hand – no less real because applying to what may be called, in a sense, a spiritual matter. So in properly laying out printing (which is nothing more than successfully designing it for a given object) it is necessary to have a certain mental equipment which is, to tell the truth, where most designers of printing fail.

This was followed by a practical and reasonable essay on type, relations with customers, and design. The enthusiast can learn much from this article, written by one of the most respected printers of his day. 'Every piece of work is different, yet each

JAN NERUDA

ZPĚVY PATEČNÍ

VYDAL

ARTHUR NOVÁK V PRAZE

1922

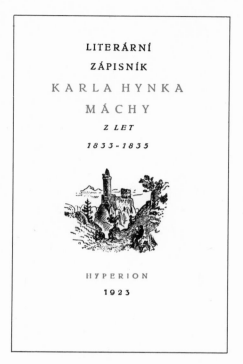

LITERÁRNÍ

ZÁPISNÍK

KARLA HYNKA

MÁCHY

Z LET

1833-1835

HYPERION

1923

IN

MEMORIAM

JIŘÍHO WOLKERA

—

Přišel jsem na svět
abych si postavil život
dle obrazu srdce svého.

—

HYPERION

V PRAZE

1924

10. *The Fleuron* No. 3:
    'Czechoslovak Printing'
    by Method Kalab.
    Left: designed by Cyril
    Bouda and printed by Kryl
    and Scotti, Novy Jičin, 1923.
    Right: designed by Cyril
    Bouda and printed by the
    Prumyslova Tiskarna,
    Prague, 1924.

is governed by common-sense illuminated by imagination. Project yourself into the situation of the user. What does he need? How does he feel? Where is he? If your design satisfies his feelings, needs and situation, you have produced printing which is suitable for its purpose.'

Stanley Morison's contribution to issue No. 2 was entitled 'Towards an Ideal Type'. He begins by commenting on the safety and strength of dogma and tradition and takes this as an opportunity to deride the experiments with letter-forms which were being carried out in Germany, 'a defect due to the absence of the strong tradition which restrains experimenters here and in America'. He traces the letter-form to the present day, praising Goudy's 'Modern' face but concluding that it is 'hardly suitable except for the more abnormal kinds of bookwork'. I do not know what Morison means by 'abnormal' but he cannot have visualised anything very extreme. He concludes with a plea:

9. *The Fleuron* No. 3:
   'Czechoslovak Printing'
   by Method Kalab.
   Designed by V. H. Brunner
   and printed by the Grafia,
   Prague, 1922.

Will not some modern designer who knows his way along the old paths fashion a fount of *maximum* homogeneity, that is to say, a type in which the upper case, in spite of its much greater angularity and rigidity, accords with the greatest fellowship of colour and form with the rounder and more vivacious lower case? So, in my submission, we shall draw nearer an ideal type.

Also in issue No. 2 was the article 'Decorated Papers' by Roger Ingpen which was very colourfully illustrated with nine tipped-in examples. One of the most striking features of *The Fleuron* was the trouble to which the editors, printers and binders went to provide extra illustration, either by tipping-in or sewing. Each volume contained examples of contemporary work and (particularly in the later numbers) specimens specially printed for *The Fleuron* as examples of type stock or presswork. This is good evidence of the esteem and respect in which Simon and Morison were held by the printing trade. The specimens were usually one-off jobs, obviously expensive and often printed abroad; their value today is beyond sensible estimation.

Issue No. 3 opens with an appreciation of D. B. Updike by W. A. Dwiggins – an article particularly notable for its illustrations, collotype reproductions of work at the Merrymount Press. Printed in three and four colours, they show the fitness of the process for reproduction of such fragile specimens – a screen would have taken the punch out of them. 'Czechoslovak Printing' by Method Kalab is also beautifully illustrated, the title pages reproduced bearing out totally the claim of the author: 'In Darel Dyrynk, editor of the journal *Typografia*, Preissig found a good collaborator, and together they raised the standard of the Czech book to an excellence which we have now grown to look for as inevitable, and to accept as an altogether necessary thing.'

Other notable items of content of the third *Fleuron* were the first of a series entitled 'Contemporary Printers' in which Frank Sidgwick wrote on Stanley Morison, with a drawing of the subject by William Rothenstein, and a set of typographical reviews to accompany the book reviews. Amongst the book reviews is one by Updike, a long view of Morison's *Four Centuries of Fine Printing*, in which it is stated that 'Mr Morison was among the few men fitted to prepare the book which is the subject of this review', and a short but glowing review, by Newdigate, of the *Catalogue Raisonné of Books Printed at the Curwen Press*, which was conceived and edited by Oliver Simon, though his name does not appear in the review. The cynical might suggest that we are dealing with a mutual appreciation society, but we should remember that Meynell, Simon, Morison, Updike, Newdigate and their colleagues and collaborators did not achieve such prestigious and enviable positions merely by using superlatives when they commented on each other's work. They were outstanding in their fields, whether they ran printing companies, designed typefaces and books or investigated printing history.

The fourth number of *The Fleuron* was the finest production yet. The subjects examined deserved, and got, lavish illustrations; Morison wrote on 'Script Types', Sidgwick on the decorations of Percy Smith, Hanna Kiel on contemporary German book-printing and Frederic Warde on the work of Bruce Rogers. Morison treats his subject in the scholarly and well-argued fashion that one would expect, but I must admit to being rather surprised to see that he quotes, several times, whole

11. *The Fleuron* No. 4: 'On Script Types' by Stanley Morison.

12. (*Overleaf, left*) *The Fleuron* No. 4: 'Tendencies in German Book Printing since 1914' by Dr Hanna Kiel. Printed by the Ernst Ludwig Press, 1921.

13. (*Overleaf, right*) *The Fleuron* No. 5: 'The Work of Karl Klingspor' by Julius Rodenberg.

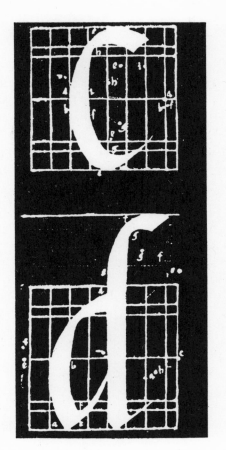

Fig. 1.—*Cancelleresca formata* from Ferdinando Ruano: *Sette Alfabeti*, Rome, 1554

Frate Vespasiano Amphyareo.

La grandißima beneuolenza qual porto al nostro commune amico, Giouan batt Ciardi. §. Christofano amantißimo, mi ha constretto di mutar proposito; impero ch sendomi quasi che deliberato di non uolere intagliare nell'opra mia altra sorte di lettra che quella Bastarda tanto fauorita, pure sapendo poi quanta inclinatione egli habbi alla mia Cancellaresca della quale tanto sollecitaua gli amati figliuolini, in sua gratificatione le presenti pollice sono date in luce, ne altro occorr se non che a V. R. et alhumanißima cortesia sua in finitamente mi Raccom.

AL suo Giouan Battista ciardj.

Fig. 2.— An early *cancelleresca bastarda* (only slightly sloped and untied) from Vespasiano Amphiareo: *Opera nella quale sinsegna a scrivere*, Venice, 1554

MATTHIAS CLAUDIUS

GEDICHTE
DES
WANDSBECKER
BOTEN

Es KOMMT IN DER KUNST NICHT DARAUF AN, DASS ETWAS GEMACHT, SONDERN DASS ETWAS AUS=GEDRÜCKT WIRD. Das Machen läßt sich mit Hilfe einer guten Schulung und einer gewissen Intelligenz erlernen. Aber die Kunst der Musik besteht nicht darin, daß man imstande ist, die Form des Walzers, der Sonate, des Liedes auszuführen mit Hilfe der künstlerischen Ideen, die Gemeingut sind, wie Luft und Licht, die Kunst der Poesie ist nicht erreicht, wenn sich einer geübt hat, Verse nach Heines Art zu verfertigen, die Kunst der Malerei hat noch nicht bewältigt, wer gelernt hat, ein Landschaftsmo=tiv oder eine Figur korrekt zu zeichnen oder zu malen. So=weit kann jeder kommen, der nicht unter dem Durchschnitt begabt ist. Von Kunst aber darf erst die Rede sein, wenn eine neue und eigene Empfindung Gestalt gewonnen hat. Das ist der Grund, weshalb so viele Bilder, die als Mache keinen Tadel verdienen, mit der Kunst nichts zu tun haben, daß so viele Musikstücke, so viele Gedichte, deren Technik nicht zu beanstanden ist, weder Musik noch Literatur sind.

paragraphs in French without providing any translation or even a hint of the context of the extract. I am not sure whether he was too generous in his assumption of his readers' education or if he was one who liked to stay one move ahead of everyone else.

At the back of issue No. 4 it is announced that the editions of Nos. 1, 2 and 3 are all out of print, but even this did not solve the financial crisis that was hanging over *The Fleuron* at the Curwen Press. Simon wrote in *Printer and Playground*: 'We were badly in need of fresh financial support. While the sale of *The Fleuron* remained satisfactory, our enthusiasms and perfectionist tendencies led us to unnecessary extravagances which might have been mitigated if we had been more experienced.' A lover of good printing might question the use of the word 'unnecessary', but it is true nevertheless that *The Fleuron* was causing a heavy financial strain on the Curwen Press; this was apparently concealed even from Oliver Simon (in the light of subsequent events this seems very likely). The time seemed right for a change.

It had been agreed in 1923 that Oliver Simon was to edit the first four numbers of *The Fleuron*, while Morison, an unpaid assistant, was vested with right of editorial succession. More than once, however, Morison was to push Simon out of the limelight; he often allowed people to believe that *The Fleuron* was his idea alone and that it exhausted his time, energy and resources. Indeed, in 1960 he made a written claim, in a draft article for the *Newberry Library Bulletin*, that he was 'working editor from the first' of *The Fleuron* and even the appointed editor of *Penrose's Annual* for three years (1923–5). The latter statement changed in the final version but the former remained. Simon's role was barely mentioned; in Moran's words 'his old friend-in-need' was reduced 'to the status of a production assistant'.[7] Yet in a nostalgic letter to Simon in 1954, Morison wrote:

> I never have any ideas of my own. You were the active man in spite of your age and bad health in the 20's and you had the Fleuron idea. I owe you a great debt, (the greatest after F. Meynell who first took me up at Burns & Oates and again at the Pelican). You immeasureably helped me with that Lund, Humphries connection and in many other ways, which I never forget. You took all the responsibility for St Stephen's House when the Cloister broke up (or down) and gave me a fine example of capacity, sense and stability. It was a very fortunate day for me when you desired my presence in your office.[8]

One is inclined to give Morison the benefit of the doubt and attribute his later claims to a hazy memory. Introducing the first issue of *The Fleuron* to D. B. Updike, he wrote, 'The credit for No. 1 belongs entirely to my colleague who also sees to the bookwork of the Curwen Press.'[9]

In 1925, Morison took up his role as typographical adviser to the Cambridge University Press and it was agreed to move the periodical to Cambridge. Herbert Simon makes an interesting point on this:

14. *The Fleuron* No. 5: 'The "Garamond" Types' by Paul Beaujon.

ALIVD ARGVMENTVM.

More captus Alcmenæ Iupiter
Mutauit fefe in formam eius coniugis,
Pro patria Amphitruo dum cernit cum hoftibus.
Mercurius ei fubferuit Sofiæ:

Fig. 15. *Robert Estienne's roman*, ante 1532: *from his Plautus:* Comediae, 1531

que dura telle perfecutiō,y eut vng nōbre merueilleux de Martirs. Mais
au bout de trois ans,elle print fin,enfēble la vie dudict Empereur, & luy
fucceda Gordian,& a Pōcian Euefque de Rome fucceda Antherus, leq̄l
aiant a peine tenu le Siege vng moys mourut, & luy fucceda Fabian,par
vne facon miraculeufe,q fut telle(ainfi q̄ lon dit) Eftant tout le Peuple
Chreftiē de Rome enfemble en Leglife,apres la mort de Antherus pour

Fig. 16. *Geofroy Tory's roman. From Eusebius:* Histoire ecclésiastique, 1532

nominis eius fyllabam,Et ille fic optime norat.hic ne ru=
fticus quidem vocem ruftice pronuntiatam agnouit. Ar=
cefilaus quom quofdam male pronuntiantes fua carmina
offendiffet,lateres illorum cōculcare cœpit.ac dicere,Vos
mea corrumpitis,ego veftra diffipabo.Quid de Fidenti=
no Martialis dicam? Carneades dicere folebat Clitoma=
chum eadem dicere,Carneadem autem eodem modo.Vi
deas ne in philofophia quidē vbi res maxime fpectantur,

Fig. 17. *Simon de Colines' larger roman of 1531. From Terentianus:* de Literis

De hortenfium femente,& quo tempore fata nafcuntur. Cap. XII.

Ementes hortenfium quibus feri fingula folent,tres omnibus
certe notátur,hyberna,æftiua,& quæ inter eas media cadit.Pri
ma poft brumā fit méfe Maio:quo brafficā,radiculam,rapum,
& quæ poftea ceu betam,lactucā,rumicem,finapi,corianum,
anethum,nafturtiū ferere confueuerunt.Secundam poft æfti=
uum folftitiū ineunte Octobri menfe præcipiunt,quū porrum

Fig. 18. *Roman and italic from Ruellius:* de Natura Stirpium, *printed by Colines in* 1536

There must have been some change of plan, for in the list of books published at The Office of The Fleuron for 1925, *The Fleuron* No. 5 edited by Stanley Morison is announced as being 'in active preparation' and was forecast to be ready in March 1926. It may well be that Morison saw that Cambridge publishing abilities and Doubleday Doran and Co. in the United States far exceeded the limited resources of The Office of The Fleuron. *Fleuron* No. 5 never appeared under the Fleuron imprint. Morison assumed sole responsibility for editorship, production and publication.[10]

After relinquishing the editorship, Simon took no further part in producing or writing *The Fleuron*. He was already deeply involved in his design and editorial work for the Curwen Press; it may be that he had come to regard *The Fleuron* as a Curwen publication and that, with the move to Cambridge, he felt under no obligation to continue working on it. The 1920s was a period of dramatic transition for Curwen, and *The Fleuron* was only one aspect of the change. The development was due almost entirely to Harold Curwen and Oliver Simon, not only their fastidiousness over seemingly small details of production but also their steadfast belief in using the best materials, be it hand-made paper or illustrations by such talented artists as Paul Nash, Eric Ravilious and Barnett Freedman. Simon was to write in 1931:

> The object of the Curwen Press is very simple. It is to give pleasure to the eventual owners of the books and, by so doing, to assure a good home for them, where they will be looked at with appreciation and taken down occasionally so that their friendliness may be felt and their pages read.[11]

If *The Fleuron* had lost a fine-spirited editor, readers could rest assured that he was doing equally important work elsewhere.

Morison was apprehensive about taking on full responsibility for *The Fleuron*. He outlined his worries in a 'Memorandum' to Frederic and Beatrice Warde, dated 10 July 1925, demonstrating the degree of hard work necessary to make the project worthwhile and mentioning other commitments that could not be put aside. 'Very seriously therefore I need much help. Nor do I know where to get it save from the two Wardes . . . The practice of working for nothing is hereby stopped. But what I want is the goods at the right time. I don't want to be told stories of Paris or Gollancz or Prunaire – or Montagnola.'[12] The last is a reference to Giovanni Mardersteig of the Officina Bodoni, with whom both Morison and Warde were very much involved at that time.

The change of editorship was not detrimental to the standard of *The Fleuron* – indeed, the last three volumes were the most lavish and 'scholarly' of all. They are of particular interest to typographers in that they were all set in Barbou type, of which Morison wrote:

Fig. 14. *Pages from the Offenbach Music Festival Programme*

15. *The Fleuron* No. 6:
'The Work of Rudolph Koch'
by Albert Windisch.

The second, and surely preferable, design [of Fournier] is numbered series 178, only one size of which, in one set of matrices, was struck. They were acquired by Cambridge, where they are known as 'Barbou', and were first used for the composition of *The Fleuron* . . . The Barbou type has had occasional use since *The Fleuron* came to its appointed end with volume VII.[13]

The binding and endpapers of issue No. 5 were designed by Emil Rudolf Weiss. That volume of *The Fleuron* was the first to include a contribution from 'Paul Beaujon', the pen-name of Beatrice Warde, soon to become editor of *The Monotype Recorder*. Her article, 'The "Garamond" Types: A study of XVI and XVII century sources', extended to fifty pages, on the first of which she defines Garamond as 'a name used by typefounders to designate an imitation of one special roman and italic owned by the Imprimerie Nationale, Paris, and called by that office *caractères de l' Université*'. She then traces the varying fortunes of the face up to its introduction for machine composition by the American and English Monotype companies, discussing the different styles in which it was designed (though she confesses that she does not know why the Linotype face is called 'Granjon'). This worthwhile piece of research is illustrated and annotated to an almost bewildering degree, although the reader should not let that deter him from a fascinating story.

Julius Rodenberg's article, 'The Work of Karl Klingspor', makes the reader all too aware that the work being done by the Nonesuch Press and the Curwen Press was much needed by English printing. The article, illustrated in several colours on fine papers, shows the work of the Klingspor Foundry through the work of its artists, notably Rudolph Koch and Walter Tiemann. Rodenberg closes on an optimistic note:

> If in conclusion we look at the work of the foundry as a whole we recognise in its many and varied manifestations one untiring effort towards the ideal, and the style of the new epoch opening out to us, which promises to bring the synthesis of artistic and technical elements, seeming to be well under way at the Klingspor Foundry. [The article is translated by Anna Simons.]

Such optimism in looking ahead is rather unusual in *The Fleuron*; its editorial success lay in its scholarship and its appreciation of the usefulness of the historical far more than in investigation of future possibilities. Stanley Morison fell early into the habit of criticising before encouraging: 'The indiscriminate stringing together of swash letters is a prevalent typographical disease . . . In typography, as in most arts and crafts, success attends the disciplined and restrained use of appropriate material.' In a later article on decorated types he asserted: 'We need founts in which the proportions and significant forms of the classic old face letters dominate the decoration.' It was a pity that he rarely encouraged experimentation – his influence might well have struck sparks of inspiration among his less gifted contemporaries.

Issue No. 6 opens with a further appreciation of Rudolph Koch, this time in an article by Albert Windisch. It touches on all aspects of Koch's work – calligraphy, typography, engraving, drawing and metalwork. As the author points out:

> The readers of *The Fleuron*, while naturally expecting some discussion of the problems of calligraphy and typography and considering as less important work which is remote from these provinces, even though it be related to them by the principles which underlie all Koch's work, may perhaps regard with sympathy any kind of work from the hand of so gifted a typographer and calligrapher as Rudolph Koch.

In fact the author does not stray from the general subject of bookwork as much as one might be led to believe. Koch's work was primarily typographic; where it was not, it was still of relevance and interest to the reader concerned mainly with book design and production.

Issue No. 6 is very much a 'foreign' volume; as well as the article on Koch there are two concerning Frenchmen – Geofroy Tory, the printer, and Bernard Naudin, illustrator – and Paul Beaujon writes on decorative printing in America. For me, however, the highlight of the number is the section of typographical reviews,

16. *The Fleuron* No. 6: 'Bernard Naudin, Illustrator' by Luc Benoist. 4pp section tipped-in.

DIDEROT

—

LE NEVEU

DE RAMEAU

AVEC

UNE NOTICE DE M. LOUIS BARTHOU
de l'Académie française

UN PORTRAIT DE DIDEROT DESSINÉ ET GRAVÉ SUR CUIVRE

PAR BERNARD NAUDIN
ET SEPT BOIS GRAVÉS DE J.-L. PERRICHON, D'APRÈS NAUDIN

ÉDITIONS D'ART ÉDOUARD PELLETAN

HELLEU ET SERGENT ÉDITEURS
125, BOULEVARD SAINT-GERMAIN, 125
À PARIS   MCMXXII

Fig. 2. *Opening pages from Diderot,* Le Neveu de Rameau (*Paris,* 1922)

which includes specially printed specimens of Jan van Krimpen's Lutetia, Emil Rudolf Weiss's Romain, Baskerville recut by the Stempel foundry, Pastonchi cut by Monotype, and Meidoorn roman designed by S. H. de Roos. The specimens include three broadsides and five booklets sewn in, one of which is the first edition of a short story by Sylvia Warner set in Pastonchi. All the specimens are printed specially for *The Fleuron*, and each face is the subject of a profound critical review, almost certainly written by Morison himself – they betray an unusual knowledge both of the history of typography and of the Lanston Monotype Corporation.

The list of contributors to issue No. 7 reads like a 'Who's Who' of twentieth-century book design; Paul Beaujon and Stanley Morison are joined by J. van Krimpen, Rudolph Koch, D. B. Updike, A. J. A. Symons and Graham Pollard. Issue No. 7 is the most extensive, the most lavish and, without a doubt, the most beautiful of all the volumes of *The Fleuron*. It also contains several major contributions to printing literature – van Krimpen's penetrating article on 'Typography in Holland'; Beaujon's essay on the work of Eric Gill and, of course, Morison's classic essay 'First Principles of Typography'. The *coup de grâce* was the inclusion of the first specimen of Gill's 'Perpetua' typeface in the form of 'The Passion of Perpetua and Felicity' with engraved illustrations also by Gill. Walter Lewis and the Cambridge University Press surpassed themselves on this job – the volume runs to nearly 300 pages with more illustrations than ever before; no wonder the editor begins by apologising for the delay in publication.

It would prove very difficult indeed to give issue No. 7 the minute attention it deserves – one could discuss Morison's 'Principles' and all the other subjects under scrutiny for a very long time and still not satisfy oneself or the reader. There is, however, another section in this number, written by Morison, which is of particular importance to this study, and that is the 'Postscript'. It begins by tracing the history of *The Fleuron* up to the change of editorship. The availability of contributions seems to have been a source of worry to Simon and Morison: 'Vague as we were, and conceited in thinking our help to be of service, the production of a first number convinced us that only a few issues would exhaust our subject so far as we, or the help available to us, could deal with it. It was decided, therefore, that *The Fleuron* should be limited to a maximum of seven numbers.' Morison writes in the following paragraph that 'the increased bulk of numbers 5, 6 and 7' was 'to some extent due to an acceptance of such moral discipline as was necessary to accomplish the job decently'. From these two claims one might be led to presume that Morison, having decided on seven issues on a finite subject, found it necessary to 'squeeze' the copy into larger volumes in order to do his job properly. I think it is more likely that Cambridge University Press were, like the Curwen Press, finding *The Fleuron* something of a burden on the smooth and profitable running of the business. I have found no indication for or against this suggestion, though James Moran suggests that Morison, in his 'ruthlessness', had grown tired of *The Fleuron* and decided to

17. *The Fleuron* No. 6: Type specimen of Meidoorn Roman by S. H. de Roos. Printed for *The Fleuron* by de Heuvelpers, Hilversum, Holland, 1927.

18. (*Overleaf, left*) *The Fleuron* No. 7: 'Eric Gill, Sculptor of Letters' by Paul Beaujon.

19. (*Overleaf, right*) *The Fleuron* No. 7: 'Eric Gill, Sculptor of Letters' by Paul Beaujon. 'The Passion of Saints Perpetua and Felicity', 32pp sewn-in.

QUID faciat lætes segetes, quo sidere terram
Vertere, Mæcenas, ulmisque adjungere vites
Conveniat: quæ cura boum, qui cultus habendo
Sit pecori, atque apibus quanta experientia parcis,
Hinc canere incipiam. Vos, o clarissima mundi
Lumina, labentem cœlo quæ ducitus annum,
Liber, et alma Ceres; vestro si munere tellus
Chaoniam pingui glandem mutavit arista,
Poculaque inventis Acheloia miscuit uvis:
Et vos agrestum præsentia numina Fauni,
Ferte simul Faunique pedem, Dryadesque puellæ:
Munera vestra cano. Tuque o, cui prima frementem
Fudit equum magno tellus percussa tridenti,
Neptune: et cultor nemorum, qui pinguia Ceæ
Ter centum nivei tondent dumeta juvenci:
Ipse nemus linquens patrium, saltusque Lycæi,
Pan ovium custos, tua si tibi Mænala curæ,
Adsis o Tegeæe favens: oleæque Minerva
Inventrix, uncique puer monstrator aratri,
Et teneram ab radice ferens, Silvane, cupressum:
Dique Deæque omnes, studium quibus arva tueri,
Quique novas alitis non ullo semine fruges:
Quique satis largum cœlo demittitis imbrem,
Tuque adeo, quem mox quæ sint habitura deorum
Concilia, incertum est; urbisne invisere, Cæsar,
Terrarumque velis curam: et te maximus orbus
Auctorem frugum tempestatumque potentem

PAUL BEAUJON

HIS HOLINESS BENEDICT POPE XV

Giacomo della Chiesa, born in Genoa, 1854, was the son of Giuseppe Marquesa della Chiesa and of Giovanna Migliorati.

The Pope's family migrated from Acqui, passed to Genoa towards the end of the fifteenth century and was admitted in 1528 to the Albergo Salviago, thereby entering the Genovan Patriarchate.

The della Chiesa bearings are, party bend sinisterwise azure and gold, a church silver roofed gules and a chief gold with an eagle sable.

Fig. 6. *Eric Gill's sans-serif upper and lower case*

necessarily sharpened angles meeting the uprights. A lower-case is now being prepared for the Gill series. Here the strictly monotone weight of the strokes has had to be set aside, but there are no obvious gradations of weight, and the result is legible and of refreshing simplicity.

As a lower-case, however, the letter does not represent that very distinctive and carefully developed alphabet which Mr Gill has been perfecting on stone for many years: an alphabet which has finally made its appearance, as the Monotype Perpetua roman and italic, a book face of the greatest importance to contemporary designers as representing perhaps the first original type-design of the twentieth century worthy of a permanent place in the history of typography.

For years it has been evident that although the process of reviving one fine old type face after another gives the typographer a wider range of styles than ever before, it must by that very richness of choice remove the incentive to develop, rather than to hark back to, traditions of the past. Faces

stature, so that he overpassed the very top of the amphi-
theatre; wearing a robe that had no girdle, with purple in
two bands running down the breast, having shoes of manifold shape in gold and silver, bearing a rod like a master of
gladiators, and a green branch whereon were golden apples.

And he besought silence and said: The Egyptian, if he shall
conquer this woman, shall slay her with the sword; and if
she shall conquer him, she shall receive this branch. And
he went away. And we came nigh to each other, and began
to buffet one another. He was fain to trip up my feet, but I
with my heels smote upon his face. And I rose up into the

bring it to a close for that more personal reason. Morison concludes his 'Postscript' by expressing his belief that *The Fleuron* had done a good job as far as it went:

> The justification for the 1,500 pages in which *The Fleuron* has discussed typography – that admittedly minor technicality of civilised life – is not the elaboration therein of any body of typographical doctrine, any simplication of the elements of arrangement, and précising of the lessons of history, though these may have been attempted; but rather its disposition to enquire and its conviction that the teaching and example of its predecessors of the English private press movement left typography, as *The Fleuron* leaves it, matter for further argument.

This would seem to imply that Morison had further similar projects in mind; in the 'Postscript' he refers to the 'task which, originally light, made during the last five years heavy demands upon the editorial leisure and means', and although it appears that he enjoyed the work, both editorial and commercial, he was to write in 1929, 'I have a very strong desire to devote my little energies to something entirely different.'[14] He clearly considered the journal a worthwhile venture, for he made several attempts to find an editorial successor and new financial backing. In 1929, he was approached with a proposal to continue *The Fleuron* himself; this was firmly rejected. The proposal came from John Holroyd Reece, a publishing entrepreneur described by Nicolas Barker as 'a creature of grandiose schemes who flashed across the typographical world like a comet'.[15] Several possibilities were discussed by Morison, Reece and van Krimpen, the last being suggested by Morison as one of the few people capable of editing the new journal. In a letter to van Krimpen in February 1931, Morison confided:

> I do not believe that Reece would organise, publish and produce *The Fleuron*. I think this: that if you were to keep everything entirely in your own hands, using him as a distributing agent and paying him on the sales effected by his organisation, he would be very glad of the arrangement, feeling that the books were a credit to him, and you would have the satisfaction that you knew where every penny of the proceeds went.[16]

In the same letter, Morison reveals that a man at the Limited Editions Club had suggested that Morison should continue *The Fleuron*. This was George Macy, founder of the Club, who offered to buy 1,500 copies of further issues and even to repay what Morison had lost in the preceding years. This scheme, like others, came to nothing.

It seems that Morison did contemplate a further journal to cover the calligraphic arts, though this scheme obviously developed no further than the initial embryonic stage.[17] The reason may be that the financial factor was too important

20. *The Fleuron* No. 7: 'First Principles of Typography' by Stanley Morison.

FIRST PRINCIPLES OF TYPOGRAPHY

by

STANLEY MORISON

Typography may be defined as the craft of rightly disposing printing material in accordance with specific purpose; of so arranging the letters, distributing the space and controlling the type as to aid to the maximum the reader's comprehension of the text. Typography is the efficient means to an essentially utilitarian and only accidentally aesthetic end, for enjoyment of patterns is rarely the reader's chief aim. Therefore, any disposition of printing material which, whatever the intention, has the effect of coming between author and reader is wrong. It follows that in the printing of books meant to be read there is little room for "bright" typography. Even dullness and monotony in the type-setting are far less vicious to a reader than typographical eccentricity or pleasantry. Cunning of this sort is desirable, even essential in the typography of propaganda, whether for commerce, politics, or religion, because in such printing only the freshest survives inattention. But the typography of books, apart from the category of narrowly limited editions, requires an obedience to convention which is almost absolute,—and with reason.

Since printing is essentially a means of multiplying, it must not only be good in itself—but good for a common purpose. The wider that purpose, the stricter are the limitations imposed upon the printer. He may try an experiment in a tract printed in an edition of 50 copies, but he shows little common sense if he experiments to the same degree in the tract having a run of 50,000. Again, a novelty, fitly introduced into a 16-page pamphlet, will be highly undesirable in a 160-page book. It is of the essence of typography and of the nature of the printed book *qua* book, that it perform a public service.

to ignore – both Curwen and Cambridge lost money on *The Fleuron* – or simply that Morison did not have the time to devote to such a difficult subject. 'The literature of printing should be extensive and learned', wrote Morison in the opening article of *The Fleuron* No. 1. Together with Oliver Simon, he was able to uphold the truth of those words to a degree that has not been superseded since. Other areas of typography called for his attention, notably Monotype and *The Times*; unlike the majority of scholars he was neither afraid nor unable to put his theory into practice.

21. *The Fleuron* No. 7:
Type specimen of Romanée
by Jan van Krimpen, cut by
Johannes Enschedé,
Haarlem, 1929.

BEATI PAULI APOSTOLI
NAUFRAGIUM, MIRACULA MELITÆ
PATRATA, ITER USQUE ROMAM,
CAPTIVITAS ROMANA

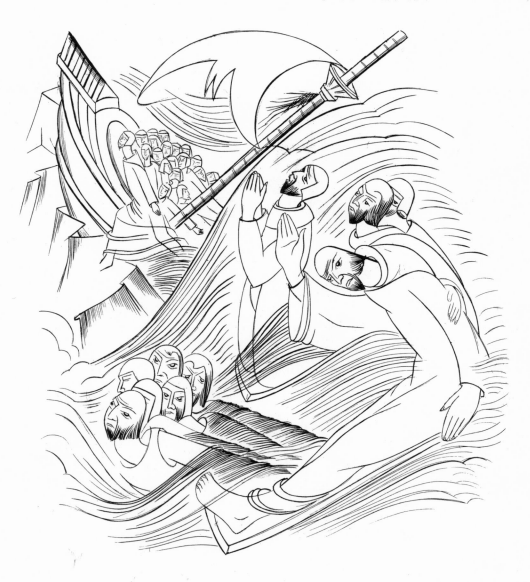

Cover of Prospectus for Golden Cockerel Press

2

Signature

OLIVER SIMON HAD AN IRREPRESSIBLE PASSION for compiling, cataloguing and editing, and it seemed inevitable that he should once again try the idea of publishing a typographical periodical. He first mentioned the project to Barnett Freedman in 1935 and met with enthusiastic encouragement. Originally, the periodical was to be called 'Impressions', but if the title changed the sub-title did not; *A Quadrimestrial of Typography and the Graphic Arts*, if a little pedantic, is an accurate description of the new publication. The subject matter was to be far more wide-ranging than that of *The Fleuron*; Simon, through his work at the Curwen Press, had met many very talented artists, and he was anxious for them to write and illustrate articles for *Signature*. Many of the most respected names in typography and art were to contribute in the years that followed: Paul Beaujon, Harry Carter, Desmond Flower, Holbrook Jackson, Ellic Howe and Stanley Morison from the printing world, and Paul Nash, John Piper, J. E. Pouterman and Graham Sutherland on the graphic side. Simon's aim, as he proclaimed in the original prospectus, was to keep the readers of *Signature* informed of the main typographic events.

Signature, printed at the Curwen Press, had a smaller format than *The Fleuron*; issued with anything from forty-eight to sixty pages, in paper-covered form, it was a far less grandiose affair. There are, however, several similarities in the design of the two periodicals, and this is due more to Simon than to the Curwen Press. Both periodicals are more reminiscent of books than journals – this fact alone links them closely with Oliver Simon, who was primarily a bookman.

The first number of *Signature* appeared in November 1935. Its contents included articles by Paul Nash, on up-and-coming artists, and by Holbrook Jackson, on John Johnson's printing collection at Oxford University Press; these were the only major articles. Oliver Simon introduced the wood-engravings of Eric Ravilious and an alphabet of initial letters by Barnett Freedman. There were two book reviews, by Harry Carter and Paul Beaujon. There was no startling new research, no provocative argument and, most important, no editorial introduction. In

22. *Signature* No. 1:
'The Printed and Published
Wood Engravings of
Eric Ravilious'
by Oliver Simon.

fifteen issues of *Signature*, the reader was to get virtually no indication of the editor's character or opinions – though the journal was owned by Simon he made no attempt to use it as a channel for his own work. As publicity for the Curwen Press, however, *Signature* was hard to beat. The production was superb: with its fine setting in Walbaum 374 and 375 (the latter is the related bold known as Walbaum Medium), printed with an evenness of colour that is rarely achieved by any printer with such consistency over a period of five years, and illustrated in anything from one to five colours, this is one of the peaks of Curwen's achievement. In fact, the production was its main attraction: the content of the first number was somewhat uninspired – the only contributors were Holbrook Jackson and Paul Nash – but issue No. 2 was much better. The best article was one written by Barnett Freedman on lithography. He recounts the invention of the process by Alois Senefelder, clearing up some of the rather vague stories and misrepresentations that had grown around that figure. He follows the process through the nineteenth century, showing the effect that photography had upon it, and hails the advent of offset printing as something of a godsend; before offset, artists were obliged to 'draw backwards' which was both difficult and inhibiting. Regarding the work of artists in this field he stresses the importance of working closely with the printer, experimenting with paper and ink, and getting to know the processes as well as possible: 'When all is said and done, nothing can take the place of an artist working in a medium which he thoroughly understands, producing works on a flat surface which go straight into the printing press, without "let or hindrance".' Freedman illustrated his article with a lithograph by Delacroix and work by the Czech artists Bouda and Svolinský, and additionally a five-colour job by Freedman himself showing the application and effect of each colour.

Issue No. 3 sees *Signature*'s first article by Stanley Morison, 'On Advertisement Settings', which argues against the prevailing trend of advertisements in the form of unbroken rectangles of type. Morison contends that 'to the lazy, tired or indifferent reader, an even grey panel of "copy", no matter in what new or old, big or little, bold or light type it is set, can never possess that instantaneous readability which is required. Legibility is not enough. We want Readability.' This seems logical enough, but what is the alternative in machine-set advertising?

> I conclude by reporting my conviction that the more cunning your illustration, the more provocative your headlines, the more necessary it is to abandon solid blocks of 10-, 11- and 12-point in favour of semi-displayed text which shall continue the momentum of interest from the displayed line over the illustration to the displayed name-block or order form at the tail.

I find it refreshing to read Morison bowing to the modern print-buyers; like Francis Meynell this essay shows Morison totally in the twentieth century, tackling real commercial problems head on.

23. *Signature* No. 3: Type specimen of Albertus Titling by Berthold Wolpe.

24. (Overleaf, left) *Signature* No. 4: 'Progress in Bible Production' by Paul Beaujon. Oxford and Cambridge University Presses 'pocket' bibles.

25. (Overleaf, right) *Signature* No. 5: 'An Introduction to Hebrew Typography' by Ellic Howe.

ABCDEFGH IJKLMNOP

ALBERTVS

SPECIMEN OF AN ALPHABET OF TITLING CAPITALS ONLY

IN **72** PT

REGISTRATION APPLIED FOR

QRSTUVW XYZ!?&M

unpleasantly condensed type is not so efficient as it would be with solid prose; there is nothing gained by cramping a verse into three full lines and one word over instead of setting four full lines in a more open, hence more legible type face. The better way is not to condense, but in effect to expand the face, that is, to choose a very open, wide-set letter and turn it from, say, a normal 10-point to a short-descender 8- or 7½-point without perceptibly reducing its 10-point legibility. Then, in the depth of 50 lines of normal-descender 10-point, one can print 62 or more lines of the smaller size. The severest test of this principle is found in the new Beryl Bible of the Oxford University Press (see Fig. 2 and caption). If we agree (as we need not) that a miniature Bible is a good thing, we can appreciate the technical brilliance of this one.

THE FIRST BOOK OF MOSES

CALLED

GENESIS

CHAPTER 1

IN the beginning God created the heaven and the earth.

2 And the earth was without form, and void; and darkness *was* upon the face of the deep. And the Spirit of God moved upon the face of the waters.

3 And God said, Let there be light: and there was light.

4 And God saw the light, that *it was* good: and God divided the light from the darkness.

5 And God called the light Day, and the darkness he called Night. And the evening and the morning were the first day.

6 ¶ And God said, Let there be a firmament in the midst of the waters, and let it divide the waters from the waters.

7 And God made the firmament, and divided the waters which *were* under the firmament from the waters which *were* above the firmament: and it was so.

8 And God called the firmament Heaven. And the evening and the morning were the second day.

9 ¶ And God said, Let the waters under the heaven be gathered together unto one place, and let the dry *land* appear: and it was so.

10 And God called the dry *land* Earth; and the gathering together of the waters called he Seas: and God saw that *it was* good.

11 And God said, Let the earth bring forth grass, the herb yielding seed, *and* the fruit tree yielding fruit after his kind, whose seed *is* in itself, upon the earth: and it was so.

12 And the earth brought forth grass, *and* herb yielding seed after his kind, and the tree yielding fruit, whose seed *was* in itself, after his kind: and God saw that *it was* good.

13 And the evening and the morning were the third day.

14 ¶ And God said, Let there be lights in the firmament of the heaven to divide the day from the night; and let them be for signs, and for seasons, and for days, and years:

15 And let them be for lights in the firmament of the heaven to give light upon the earth: and it was so.

16 And God made two great lights; the greater light to rule the day, and the lesser light to rule the night: *he made* the stars also.

17 And God set them in the firmament of the heaven to give light upon the earth,

18 And to rule over the day and over the night, and to divide the light from the darkness: and God saw that *it was* good.

19 And the evening and the morning were the fourth day.

20 And God said, Let the waters bring forth abundantly the moving creature that hath life, and fowl *that* may fly above the earth in the open firmament of heaven.

21 And God created great whales, and every living creature that moveth, which the waters brought forth abundantly, after their kind, and every winged fowl after his kind: and God saw that *it was* good.

22 And God blessed them, saying, Be fruitful, and multiply, and fill the waters in the seas, and let fowl multiply in the earth.

23 And the evening and the morning were the fifth day.

24 ¶ And God said, Let the earth bring forth the living creature after his kind, cattle, and creeping thing, and beast of the earth after his kind: and it was so.

25 And God made the beast of the earth after his kind, and cattle after their kind, and every thing that creepeth upon the earth after his kind: and God saw that *it was* good.

26 ¶ And God said, Let us make man in our image, after our likeness: and let them have dominion over the fish of the sea, and over

5

Fig. 3

THE FIRST BOOK OF MOSES,

CALLED

GENESIS.

CHAPTER 1.

IN the beginning God created the heaven and the earth.

2 And the earth was without form, and void; and darkness *was* upon the face of the deep. And the Spirit of God moved upon the face of the waters.

3 And God said, Let there be light: and there was light.

4 And God saw the light, that *it was* good: and God divided the light from the darkness.

5 And God called the light Day, and the darkness he called Night. And the evening and the morning were the first day.

6 ¶ And God said, Let there be a firmament in the midst of the waters, and let it divide the waters from the waters.

7 And God made the firmament, and divided the waters which *were* under the firmament from the waters which *were* above the firmament: and it was so.

8 And God called the firmament Heaven. And the evening and the morning were the second day.

9 ¶ And God said, Let the waters under the heaven be gathered together unto one place, and let the dry *land* appear: and it was so.

10 And God called the dry *land* Earth; and the gathering together of the waters called he Seas: and God saw that *it was* good.

11 And God said, Let the earth bring forth grass, the herb yielding seed, *and* the fruit tree yielding fruit after his kind, whose seed *is* in itself, upon the earth: and it was so.

12 And the earth brought forth grass, *and* herb yielding seed after his kind, and the tree yielding fruit, whose seed *was* in itself, after his kind: and God saw that *it was* good.

13 And the evening and the morning were the third day.

14 ¶ And God said, Let there be lights in the firmament of the heaven to divide the day from the night; and let them be for signs, and for seasons, and for days, and years:

15 And let them be for lights in the firmament of the heaven to give light upon the earth: and it was so.

16 And God made two great lights; the greater light to rule the day, and the lesser light to rule the night: *he made* the stars also.

17 And God set them in the firmament of the heaven to give light upon the earth,

18 And to rule over the day and over the night, and to divide the light from the darkness: and God saw that *it was* good.

19 And the evening and the morning were the fourth day.

20 And God said, Let the waters bring forth abundantly the moving creature that hath life, and fowl *that* may fly above the earth in the open firmament of heaven.

21 And God created great whales, and every living creature that moveth, which the waters brought forth abundantly, after their kind, and every winged fowl after his kind: and God saw that *it was* good.

22 And God blessed them, saying, Be fruitful, and multiply, and fill the waters in the seas, and let fowl multiply in the earth.

23 And the evening and the morning were the fifth day.

24 ¶ And God said, Let the earth bring forth the living creature after his kind, cattle, and creeping thing,

5

Fig. 4

אמר ר׳ יצחק לא היה צריך להתחיל
את התורה אלא מהחדש הזה לכם
שהיא מצוה ראשונה שנצטוו ישראל
ומה טעם פתח בבראשית משום כח

Type used for the first book printed in Hebrew. (*A Commentary on the Pentateuch*.) Reggio di Calabria, 1475

וְכַפְתֹּר תַּחַת שְׁנֵי הַקָּנִים מִמֶּנָּה וְכַפְתֹּר
תַּחַת שְׁנֵי הַקָּנִים מִמֶּנָּה וְכַפְתֹּר תַּחַת
שְׁנֵי הַקָּנִים מִמֶּנָּה לְשֵׁשֶׁת הַקָּנִים הַיֹּצְאִים
מִן הַמְּנֹרָה: כַּפְתֹּרֵיהֶם וּקְנֹתָם
מִמֶּנָּה יִהְיוּ כֻּלָּהּ מִקְשָׁה אַחַת זָהָב
טָהוֹר: וְעָשִׂיתָ אֶת נֵרֹתֶיהָ שִׁבְעָה וְהֶעֱלָה
אֶת נֵרֹתֶיהָ וְהֵאִיר עַל עֵבֶר פָּנֶיהָ:

Type of Gerson Soncino, cut *circa* 1491

דברים שאין להם שיעור הפאה והבכורים
והראיון וגמילות חסדים ותלמוד תורה אילו
דברים שאדם אוכל פידותיהן בעולם הזה
והקרן קיימת לו לעולם הבא כבוד אב ואם
וגמילות חסד׳ והבאת שלום בין אדם לחבירו
ותלמוד תורה כנגד כולם: אין

Type of Daniel Bomberg, Venice, cut *circa* 1540

Also in this issue of *Signature* was Monotype's first specimen of Berthold Wolpe's Albertus Titling. A four-page inset shows the new face (cut only in the 72-point size) that was to become one of the most popular display faces. Among the shorter book reviews is one of Jan Tschichold's *Typographische Gestaltung*: his ideas were still being received with little or no emotion; the unnamed reviewer admits a certain respect for the great typographer but implies a belief that Tschichold is a little immature.

Issue No. 4 contains an article entitled 'Progress in Bible Production' by Paul Beaujon. Beaujon was one of *Signature*'s best contributors – the articles were always interesting, always well written and well illustrated, and consistently faithful to the periodical's aim of keeping its readers informed. This one on bible production is particularly good; the illustrations include insets of two of the finest bibles to be printed in modern times – Bruce Rogers' Oxford Lectern Bible and the new Enschedé Bible designed by J. van Krimpen in Monotype Times New Roman – and also show the respective 'pocket' bibles of Oxford and Cambridge University Presses. Also in this number was an article by Kenneth Clark entitled 'A Note on Three Illustrations to *Wuthering Heights*', which compares three pictures of the same subject and cites Graham Sutherland's drawing as the most distinguished. An article by A. F. Johnson provides a comprehensive survey of the typographic and calligraphic studies of Stanley Morison. The list is exceptionally useful as it divides Morison's work up by subject rather than by chronology.

Never daunted by the unusual, and indeed often positively attracted to it, Simon included in issue No. 5 an article by Ellic Howe on Hebrew typography, which examines Hebrew types and especially those cut and used in Western Europe. Apparently the first specimen of Hebrew printing in Europe appeared in a book printed by Wynkyn de Worde in 1524 in which only a few Hebrew words occur. The type was roughly cut on wood. Howe, himself a Jew, was pleased to see renewed interest in the printing of the language: 'Now that Hebrew is again a living language, there may be a revival for the better in Hebrew type design.' Amongst the book reviews was one by Francis Meynell on Eric Gill's *An Essay on Typography*; Meynell admitted to being a long-standing admirer of Gill's work but still found the book rather impractical and self-contradictory. A review that appeared in *Typography* at this time (summer 1937) compared Gill's book unfavourably with Morison's *First Principles of Typography*.

In an article called 'They March with Banners' in issue No. 6, H. S. Williamson looks at art and typographical periodicals from 1890 to 1930. Beginning with the 'Art Nouveau' magazines of the pre-war period, the article finishes with the end of *The Fleuron*. Williamson gives a bombastic but highly favourable opinion of that periodical:

26. *Signature* No. 6: 'René Ben Sussan' by J. E. Pouterman.

To convey any idea of what sumptuousness of production, what varied interest,

Wood-engraving from *L'Immoraliste* (Jonquières)

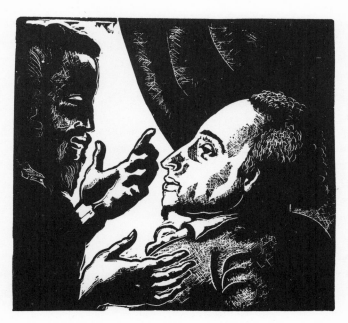

Wood-engraving for projected edition of Israel Zangwill's
Children of the Ghetto

THE MERCHANT
OF VENICE

by William Shakespeare

London: J. M. DENT & SONS LTD.
New York: E. P. DUTTON & CO. INC.

THE MERCHANT OF VENICE

I would not have given it for a wilderness of monkeys.

Tub. But Antonio is certainly undone.

Shy. Nay, that's true, that's very true. Go, Tubal, fee me an officer, bespeak him a fortnight before, I will have the heart of him if he forfeit, for were he out of Venice I can make what merchandise I will. Go, 120 Tubal, and meet me at our synagogue; go, good Tubal, at our synagogue, Tubal. *Exeunt*

SCENE II

Belmont.   A room in Portia's house

Enter Bassanio, Portia, Gratiano, Nerissa, and Attendants

Por. I pray you tarry, pause a day or two
Before you hazard, for, in choosing wrong,
I lose your company; therefore forbear awhile.
There's something tells me (but it is not love)
I would not lose you, and you know yourself,
Hate counsels not in such a quality.
But lest you should not understand me well,—
And yet a maiden hath no tongue, but thought,—
I would detain you here some month or two
Before you venture for me. I could teach you   10

58

what scholarship and what standard of aesthetic control was provided under the simple sub-title 'A Journal of Typography' and to express it in a paragraph would baffle the commentator, much as if the ghosts of Ictinus and Callicrates were to approach the amiable traveller and invite from him a word of kindly comment on their Parthenon.

27. *Signature* No. 7: 'Some Recent Editions of Shakespeare's Works' by Paul Beaujon.

28. *Signature* No. 8: 'The Ampersand – Sign of Continuity' by Paul Standard.

The author goes on in ever more flowering language:

Happily unlike those periodicals whose first number is the most memorable and whose end is obscure *The Fleuron* always seemed to march from strength to strength, and in the final number attained a size and a magnificence which seemed to mark the end, not of a periodical whose vitality had failed, but of one which, through an unrestricted flow, poured out in ever-increasing abundance, had left no more to be said than 'We have achieved'.

The article contains no reference to Simon's editorship, or to the value of *Signature* itself; perhaps here we are given a glimpse of the man behind these periodicals, who in his modesty erased his name from Williamson's article without subtracting any honour from Morison's name.

In his autobiography, *Printer and Playground*, Simon reveals that one thousand copies of each of the first six numbers of *Signature* were printed and that by 31 August 1937 (No. 6 appeared in July) the sales were as follows: No. 1 – 627 copies, No. 2 – 575, No. 3 – 564, No. 4 – 481, No. 5 – 450, and No. 6 – 444 copies sold. Simon comments:

ENGLAND

Beauchesne and Baildon
1571

| Anon | Billingsly | Browne | Hodder | Cocker | Elder | Seddon | Seddon |
| 1590 | 1618 | 1638 | 1659 | 1661 | 1695 | 1695 | 1700 |

Ayres   Shelley
1700   1710

| Shelley | Snell | Olyffe | Bickham | Bland | Tomkins |
| 1710 | 1712 | 1713 | 1741 | 1760 | 1777 |

| Johnston | Morison | Stone | Hewitt | Fairbank | Symons |
| 1909 | 1936 | 1935 | 1935 | 1936 | 1936 |

THE NETHERLANDS

Mercator
1540

It soon became apparent that those who subscribed through an interest in the graphic arts were not necessarily equally interested in contemporary art and vice versa. We nevertheless held to our course and as time went on there was both a gradual sale of back numbers and a further decline of support for each number as it was published. However, for the next eight numbers the quantity printed was reduced to 750 copies. As time went on we were fortunate to discover some excellent new contributors and fresh subject-matter.[1]

Simon's diagnosis of the disappointing sales figures was in all probability correct; no one could complain of the price of *Signature*, at three shillings per number. Herbert Simon suggests that the journal would have sold equally well at four times the price.[2]

The next two numbers were not as good as their predecessors, though the production quality was as superb as ever. In No. 7, Paul Beaujon wrote on 'Some Recent Editions of Shakespeare's Works' in which she praised the new Penguin editions that had just been published. No. 8 saw a good article on the calligraphic ampersand by Paul Standard. Issue No. 9 was a great improvement; there was a good amount of original material on a variety of subjects, including a study by James Wardrop of the great eighteenth-century papermaker, James Whatman, and one by Peggy Laing on 'Swelled Rules and Typographic Flourishes'. Most important was Desmond Flower's contribution 'A Survey of Modern Binding', illustrated with collotypes. Of English binding, Flower wrote: 'There is little to choose between the best trade bindings produced in this country by such publishers as Mr de la Mare and the artists working under his direction, and the best work of Germany and the United States. But it is in the general level, the quantity, that we are far surpassed by the other countries.' Flower nominates Ignaz Wiemeler as 'undoubtedly the greatest binder in the world today'. In his conclusion, he sees the 'depression' in English bookbinding as one of personality rather than economics: 'Here, indeed, is our great lack at the present time in England: one brilliant man who, by his example, may infuse life and confidence into the bookbinders of this country. . . . They say a boxer never comes back; I wonder if a bookbinder can.' Perhaps Flower's forecast was somewhat pessimistic, but as co-editor of *The Book Collector's Quarterly* he was qualified to assess the state of English bookbinding.

Issue No. 10 (November 1938) was remarkable not in itself but in the number of important and influential books that were reviewed in that number, which included Stanley Morison's *The Art of Printing*, Holbrook Jackson's *The Printing of Books* and Bernard Newdigate's *The Art of the Book*. The following number contained an article by Stanley Morison called 'Leipzig as a Centre of Typefoundry'. Uncharacteristically, he strays from his subject and concludes that:

A Song about Tsar Ivan Vasilyevitch by Lermontov. Light red morocco, inlaid black and ivory niger, tooled in blind, designed by Paul Nash for the Aquila Press, 1929

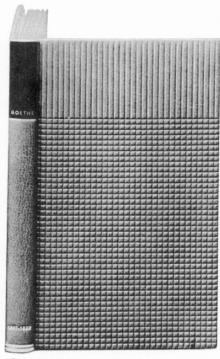

Goethe, 1807–1832. Cinnamon red goatskin, inlaid black, and tooled in gold and blind, by Ignaz Wiemeler, 1931

29. *Signature* No. 9:
'A Survey of Modern
Binding'
by Desmond Flower.
Printed by collotype.

. . . the justification for printing is not primarly stylistic; first and foremost its justification is economic. . . . Indeed, it seems to the present writer not too much to say, regarding book typography in the period after Garamond and Granjon that it is in the exploitation of the available space, rather than in conspicuous details such as serifs and stresses, there lies the secret of successful type design.

Morison is the star of issue No. 12 as it was the occasion of his fiftieth birthday; the event is celebrated in *Signature* by the printing of a new portrait of him by a young artist named Frances MacDonald. Also in No. 12 was an article about the Pelican Press, between 1916 and 1923, by Philip James; he makes valuable comment on the importance and success of the Press:

30. (Overleaf, left)
Signature No. 10:
'Henry Fuseli RA 1741–1825'
by John Piper.

31. (Overleaf, right)
Signature No. 11:
'Leipzig as a Centre of
Typefoundry'
by Stanley Morison.

. . . it remains an incontestable fact that, by its success in accepting the principle of machine printing and at the same time introducing something new in the way of richness and decoration the Pelican Press not only gave delight in a starved and war-weary world, but was a powerful influence in the moulding of contemporary commercial typography.

FUSELI: SHAKESPEARE PARTY (pen drawing)
(*Reproduced by permission of Thomas Lowinsky*)

UBI NON EST VICTUS,
IBI CESSAT. Œ Q J

UNA HORA, IN QUA FRUI-
TURI SVMVS RECREA-
TIONE VITÆ. & Œ. J.

NON EST IN MANIBUS NOSTRIS
FORTUNA MALORUM, NEQUE
CASTIGATIO JUSTOR. & Œ J

NE CUPIAS PROXIMUM TUUM VIDERE,
EO TEMPORE CUM VILIS HABETUR &
IGNOMINIÆ EXPONITUR. Œ Q J

EO QUOD ALIOS SIC NATARE FECISTI, TE QUO-
QUE NATARE FACIENT, & FINIS EORUM, QUI
TE NATARE FACIUNT, ERIT, UT. Œ J

AD FACIENDUM VOLUNTATEM DEI SIS ANIMOSUS
SICUT PARDUS, LEVIS SICUT AQUILA, CELER
SICUT CAPREA, & FORTIS SICUT LEO. Œ J

TRIA CONSIDERA, & NON INCIDES IN TRANSGRESSIONEM,
SCIAS, QUOD SUPRA TE SIT; OCULUS VIDENS, AURIS
AUDIENS, & QUOD OMNES ACTIONES TUÆ IN
LIBRO ANNOTENTUR. Œ J

Daß obgeſetzter Schrifften Prob und Abgüß in der Lutheriſchen Schrifft-Gieſſerey zu
Franckfurt am Mayn um die Gebühr zu bekommen ſeynd/ ſolches hat man denen
Buchdruckern hiedurch bekant machen wollen. 1716.

Fig. 4.—The Luther Specimen (Frankfurt/M., 1716) showing condensed bold titling capitals.

By the time issue No. 13 appeared, the Second World War had broken out. Simon wrote in his autobiography: 'Our first reaction was to cease publication forthwith, but after reflections on former wars I decided to attempt to finish the series as well as circumstances would permit, complete with an Index.'[3] I find the dropping of the editorial 'we' very interesting. It shows that this decision was made by Simon alone and that he felt very deeply about it. He was encouraged, he says, by precedent, in that some of the greatest printing jobs had been achieved during war 'when circumstances were distressing to say the least'.

The first wartime *Signature* is not an outstanding one; it is unusual, even surprising, in that it contains an article entitled 'Cheltenham' – one's first reaction might be that the article had found its way into the wrong journal. In fact, 'Cheltenham' is about architecture and is illustrated with a large fold-out lithograph by John Piper which is half-map, half-painting of the town.

Issue No. 14 is a particularly interesting one as it contains an article by J. E. Pouterman on books illustrated by Pablo Picasso. Actually, it is more of a list than an article, though the brief introduction is fascinating; in it the author recounts the impressions of a mutual friend of himself and Picasso: 'Absentmindedly he would listen to his visitors, all the time staring at the corner stacked with tubes of paint. He seemed continually conscious of the many surfaces still waiting to be covered with paint. One felt, somehow, that Pablo was impatient to lay bare the entrails of the world.' Most of Picasso's book-illustrations were in monochrome line, as the small selection of examples showed. The hand-list of books extends to forty-six, and is supplemented with a further four by Picasso himself. The reason that Pouterman's list is incomplete is provided by an obituary at the beginning of the number: 'We deeply regret to announce that Mr J. E. Pouterman died early in February, just a few days after he had completed the Picasso article and hand-list printed in this number.'[4]

Issue No. 15 appeared late in December 1940. It was rather short of copy and perhaps the most interesting article is 'Napoleon's Books' by Desmond Flower, which is very refreshing for its slightly humorous approach. It seems that Napoleon was a bibliophile in the grand manner:

During his ten years' reign Napoleon assembled on his own shelves over seventy thousand volumes, ranging from editions de luxe produced under his patronage to small volumes assembled for his distraction while on active service. Each one of them was bound by a craftsman of the first rank.

If Europe lost by Napoleon's ambitions, it seems to have gained by his extravagant tastes: 'As the Emperor read constantly on his campaigns and threw what he did not like out of the window of his coach, many of the libraries of Europe possess

32. *Signature* No. 12: 'The Pelican Press 1916–23' by Philip James.

33. (Overleaf, left) *Signature* No. 14: 'Books Illustrated by Pablo Picasso, by J.E. Pouterman.

34. (Overleaf, right) *Signature* No. 15: 'Anton Janson Identified' by Stanley Morison.

A PRINTER'S
Miscellany

❦

THIS is the first sheet of a diminutive and very informal monthly. Good advertising of a thing he must buy has a keen interest for every business man: so we shall not try to cover up the fact that "A Printer's Miscellany" is planned to advertise the printing of the Pelican Press. It is planned to do more: both by its manner and its matter to advertise the whole cause of better printing. Curious old items such as that we print on page 4; modern asides of the lay-out department; the kind of technicality useful to appraisers of printing—these will fill its pages, or, indeed, its page: for we have a modest idea of the time we can filch from a busy man; and we, besides, are too full of our customers' work to enlarge our own.

This page is set, to accord with the matter on the fourth page, in the 17th century style of English printing. Of that time are the initial and the "flower" border. Period Printing is a particular delight of the Pelican Press; for it alone amongst the presses of this country has type and borders, ornaments and initials appropriate to all the most significant moments in the history of typography; appropriate also to every need of the publisher and advertiser to-day.

Please keep for the subsequent parts the folder in which this is contained.

[When

A page from the first number of *A Printer's Miscellany*

Fig. 1

Fig. 2

Fig. 3

Fig. 4

Figs. 1 and 2. Initial letters reproduced from designs by Geofroy Tory in the early sixteenth century.

Figs. 3 and 4 engraved on wood after Italian originals.

Illustration from *Les Metamorphoses.* See item No. 33

Lebens-Lauff.

ES ist der Wohl-Ehrenveste und Kunstreiche Herr Anthon Janson/ weitberühmter Schriftgießer athier/ von Christlichen wiewohl reformirten Eltern zu Wauden in Frießland Anno 1620. auf dem Anthonius-Tag/ war der 17. Januarii auf diese Welt gebohren worden. Sein Vater ist gewesen ein ehrlicher und wohlhabender Bauers-Mann daselbst/ nahmens Johann Dieterich Janson; Die Mutter aber nahmens Lolche Thomis gebohrne Eissens. Gleichwie nun diese seine Eltern sich über diesen von GOtt bescherten Ehe-Segen von Hertzen erfreuet; also haben sie auch alsobald des andern Tages darauf diesen ihren lieben Sohn zu dem Bad der H. Tauffe nach der reformirten Gebrauch befördert. Hernach auch/ so bald sich nur der Verstand bey ihm hervor gethan/ haben sie an guter Auferziehung/ und Anhaltung zur Schule nichts ermangeln lassen; Weil sie aber schon in seiner blühenden Jugend große Liebe und Begierde zu allerley Kunst bey ihm vermercket/ haben sie ihn auf Einrathung seiner damahligen Præceptoren und anderer verständigen Leute in dem 15. Jahre seines Alters/ nemlich Anno 1635. nach der weltberühmten Stadt Amsterdam zu einen Kunstreichen und berühmten Schriftgießer in die Lehre verdinget; welche rühmliche Kunst er denn innerhalb 6. Jahren also gefasset/ daß sein ietzt belobter Lehr-Herr ein dergestalt sattsames Vergnügen darüber gehabt/ daß er ihn als einen Factor über seine gantze Schriftgießerey setzen wollen. Weil er aber eine sonderbare Begierde bey sich verspüren ließe/ fremde Länder und Städte zu besehen/ hat ihm gedachter Lehr-Herr solches nicht mißgönnen wollen/ sondern ihm/ nachdem er noch etliche Jahr bey ihm verharret/ und sich ie mehr und mehr perfectioniret/ der Kunst Gebrauch nach mit einem guten und gültigen Lehr-Brief versehen/ und ihm den Segen Gottes und alles Wohlergehen auf seine Reise gewünschet. Da er denn Anno 1651. nach Franckfurt am Mayn sich gewendet/ daselbst seine Kunst rühmlich fortgesetzet/ und sich also damit herfür gethan/ daß auch ein

Fig. 1. First page of the funeral discourse on Anton Janson
(From the Stolberg-Stolberg Coll., Leipzig)

copies of sumptuously bound novels or classics in small format which were once carefully picked up from the roadside.'

Issue No. 15 was to be the last of the series. Curiously, this number was entirely made up in double column. Simon provides an 'Editor's Note':

> The current number of *Signature* is the last for the time being. We have decided to suspend publication until after the war. Many of our contributors are in His Majesty's forces or are working in war departments of the various Ministries. Furthermore, many of the great libraries are temporarily closed or partly closed. Of the artists whose work has appeared in *Signature*, Edward Ardizzone, Edward Bawden, Evelyn Dunbar, Barnett Freedman, Frances MacDonald, Paul Nash, John Piper, Eric Ravilious and Graham Sutherland have become official war artists. In these circumstances our readers will, no doubt, concur with our decision.[5]

Simon's decision was reinforced by the Luftwaffe. He recounts the story:

> The last number of *Signature* nevertheless eventually went to press. On the night of 7 October 1940 when it was on the machine, a bomb fell on the Curwen Press, which destroyed the directors' and administrative offices. The blast removed all the glass from the machine-room roof, which took some days to restore. The weather remained fine and dry and the final number of *Signature*, a mere 550 copies, was printed under a bright blue sky.[6]

Simon was true to his word and the first number of *Signature* New Series, as it was called, appeared in July 1946. This is outside the period I have chosen to examine but it is a useful document in that Simon lists in it the men who had died since 1940 'who each in his own way was concerned with "The Art of the Book"'. The list is a depressingly long one, but it includes Douglas Cockerell (binder), Eric Gill (artist and type designer), C. H. St John Hornby (Ashendene Press), Edward Johnston (calligrapher), Bernard Newdigate (Shakespeare Head Press), Carl Ernst Poeschel (Poeschel and Trepte), Eric Ravilious (artist), Daniel Berkeley Updike (Merrymount Press), Emil Rudolf Weiss (artist and type designer) and Rex Whistler (artist).[7] Truly this was the end of an age.

If *Signature* had a fault, it was that the content was weighted too much in favour of the historical rather than the contemporary. It is noticeable that in the last few numbers, the journal became less of a typographical periodical than one more closely related to arts and crafts. This is not to invite indifference towards the journal – it was excellent in its own way, but its production at the Curwen Press meant that the art of the illustrator rather than the craft of the printer was likely to become the more prominent theme. Nevertheless, *Signature* has a quality of design and production which few printers were capable of achieving. The rise of the Curwen Press is one of the great printing phenomena of this century; from being a small music publisher it quickly moved into a position of·ever-increasing prominence and now enjoys the reputation of being one of the finest printing houses in the world. Simon played no small part in that sudden rise, and this fact alone makes *Signature* a journal deserving of examination and praise.

Oliver Simon's contribution to printing literature cannot be valued too highly. As well as founding and editing two remarkable periodicals he wrote one of the classical textbooks still referred to by printers, editors and designers many years after its first appearance. *Introduction to Typography* (first published in 1945) may be recommended to anyone interested in this most absorbing of subjects, written by one of the most distinguished printers of his time.

TO-DAY at the LONDON PAVILION

CLARK GABLE

LORETTA YOUNG & JACK OAKIE

in Jack London's Klondyke classic

" CALL OF THE WILD "

     The call of gold and of a
girl . . .

" If there's anything you need—
grab it. That's the law of the
Klondyke. It's a good law. It
works."

A Darryl Zanuck 20th Century production presented by Joseph M. Schenck.
Also Walt Disney's Silly Symphony "The Golden Touch."

Today at 10.0; 12.15; 2.30; 4.45; 7.0; And at 9.15 a Gala Performance
(tickets 10s. 6d. to £10.10.0) in aid of German Jewish refugees.

UNITED ARTISTS   Cert. "A"

•**Charles Laughton** as the
ruthless detective; **Fredric
March** as his poignant victim;
Cedric Hardwicke as the
good Bishop Bienvenu; in
LES MISERABLES
Victor Hugo's classic story —
the most thrilling **man-hunt**
which human genius has yet
imagined or enacted.
•**TO-DAY—at the TIVOLI**

A 20th Century production. Joseph M. Schenck presents it. DARRYL ZANUCK
produces it. United Artists distributes it. Cert. A.

(A Gaumont-British Theatre)

Typewriter for Mr. Gable, and for Mr. Laughton
a typographical medley reminiscent
of Mr. Gollancz at his
miscellaneous and sabbatical best

3

Typography

THE DIFFERENCE between *Typography*, which first appeared in 1936, and *The Fleuron* is striking. Editorially, *Typography* is much fresher; it is more optimistic and more comprehensive; issue No. 1 includes an article on 'Kardomah Tea Labels' by Bernard Griffin, and issue No. 2 one entitled 'Tram Ticket Typography' by J. C. Allsop, hardly subjects that one can imagine Stanley Morison including in one of his publications. *Typography* looks to the future rather than into the past, seeing potential in experiment rather than triviality. Visually the change is even more marked; the bulky clothbound volumes of *The Fleuron* could scarcely be more different from the forty-eight-page, paper-covered, plastic-comb-bound editions of *Typography*. The text was made up in two and three columns, with illustrations well integrated with the text. Each article was designed individually, making the journal visually appealing to those who might otherwise find little interest in it. Like the editors of *The Imprint*, the editors of *Typography* had aims of the most generous and useful kind; in the introductory note of issue No. 1, Robert Harling wrote:

> We are neither atavistic nor *avantgarde*, neither traditionists nor traducers of tradition. We are, quite simply, contemporary . . . It is our hope and belief that *Typography* will prove to be the most stimulating and welcome journal of typography in England; acknowledging sound traditions; welcoming adventurous use of new materials and new forms; not afraid to accuse the stagnant traditionist or to condemn the spurious modernist.[1]

This carried strong echoes of *The Imprint*'s claim that 'our policy is sincerely to improve the craft of which we are so proud'; *Typography* went further by investigating printing of all kinds and not just book-printing. In the prospectus was the statement: 'The sponsors of *Typography* believe that fine book production is not the only means of typographical expression or excitement. We believe, in fact,

35. *Typography* No. 1: 'Voices and Vices' by Francis Meynell. Advertisements for Clark Gable and Charles Laughton.

that a bill-head can be as aesthetically pleasing as a bible, that a newspaper can be as typographically arresting as a Nonesuch.'[2]

Although the introductory notes were attributed to three men, Robert Harling was sole editor of *Typography*. His close friend and partner James Shand was responsible for publication and, as managing director of the Shenval Press, Shand was able to make a major contribution to the finished product. Robert Harling has referred to him as 'the most co-operative, generous, venturesome and full-hearted printer any editor has ever had'.[3] Ellic Howe, then only twenty-five years old, was already an acknowledged authority on the history of printing. He appears to have acted only in an advisory capacity for Harling – in the few books that mention *Typography*, there is no reference to Howe, nor anything that might suggest that the editorial work was carried out by anyone but Harling. Howe's contributions to the journal were all concerned with the history of printing, while Harling's and Shand's were modern in every respect. After the first issue, Howe severed his editorial connection with *Typography* while continuing to contribute material to the journal.

'Voices and Vices' by Francis Meynell, the opening article of issue No. 1, was about the typography of film publicity. He decides that the advertiser has to provide 'enough novelty to catch the eye, enough conventionality to fulfil the expectation; and then what you will of charm or dynamite to the whole boiling'. Writing on the technical difficulties involved, like printing on newsprint at high speed, Meynell himself is both charming *and* dynamic. Earlier, referring to design, he compares cinema advertising design with the design of postage stamps, a comparison to my mind rather simplistic – advertising has a specific function, while a stamp is little more than a receipt. Meynell did much publicity work for Gaumont-British and United Artists, and it surprises me that such an experienced man should suggest such a similarity. His conclusion, however, is a fine one, for it points out a fault in many modern marketing campaigns, for books as well as films: 'We should promote a habit and an expectation of enjoyment. Individual pictures are nearly always over-sold; what is under-sold is "going to *the pictures*".' It was this kind of article and this kind of conclusion that gave the sponsors of *Typography* good reason to call themselves 'contemporary'.

Two articles in particular, written by Harling and Shand themselves, carried on this contemporary, up-to-date editorial policy. Shand's, entitled 'The Alphabet and the Printing Press', is a plea for a rethink of typographical traditions. The author comes up with some sparkling and thought-provoking opinions:

The format of multi-edition daily newspapers must be subject to the physical necessities of immediate distribution, yet their typography represents the daily reading habits of millions of people . . . The conventions of the printed book may have settled down in the sixteenth century, but it is difficult to appreciate why

36. *Typography* No. 2: 'Slug' by James Shand. Set in Linotype Estienne.

37. (Overleaf, left) *Typography* No. 3: 'Type Mixtures' by Jan Tschichold.

38. (Overleaf, right) *Typography* No. 3: Type specimen of Egmont by S. H. de Roos.

OSCAR WILDE
RECOLLECTIONS BY
JEAN PAUL RAYMOND
& CHARLES RICKETTS

THE NONESUCH PRESS
BLOOMSBURY MCMXXXII

ROMAN CAPITALS

we mix, of course, with lower-case letters
in the same typographical family

Large lower-case italics

can be mixed with Roman,
but never mix old style and modern

Extra Bold Sans

can be used with medium
or light weights of the same family

Fat-face types

can be used with modern types
but not with old style

Bolder Egyptian

with lighter Egyptian types
in small quantities

Fat-face italics

can be used with modern types such as
Walbaum, Bodoni or Scotch Roman

Copperplate Scripts

can be used with Typewriter type
or with lighter Egyptian types

Parisian Ronde

can be mixed with modern types:
Walbaum or Scotch Roman

Condensed Sans types

should only be used with smaller
or lighter variations of the same family

Bold face is not used very often in books, but there is no reason why books set in a pronounced modern style should not have these bold variations introduced into the body matter for emphasis.

Types for title-pages of books can be the same as that used for the body matter. If one has confined oneself to roman and italic, one will set the title-page, or at least the main line, in letter-spaced capitals, which are at once pleasing æsthetically and easy to read. Or they can contrast with the body type, which is not so frequently done: for example, *Old Black* for the title-page with *Garamond* for the body.

Already in books of modern character, where headlines are not centred but ranged left or right, a suitable *Egyptian* can be used for the headlines and title in conjunction with the roman text and its accompanying italic. Not more than one entirely different fount should be used with the text types. For example: a medium bold *Egyptian*, in no more than two sizes, would be in order with *Garamond* roman and italic as text type. When a display face is being set, account must be taken of the nature of the copy; but in spite of this, there is no necessity to fit the choice of type in every case to the literary content of the book.

This rule should also be observed in advertisement and jobbing setting. But here far more contrasting mixtures can be used than in books. The examples of type mixtures accompanying this article show a variety of possible combinations. They are only a small selection from an abundance of possibilities; they show, above all, types that are congenial to contemporary taste.

Type mixtures have an important bearing on the development of contemporary typography: they suggest a number of new possibilities which are individual to each printing office, since each office has different types. Type mixing has also in these days an increasing significance, because with its aid, interesting effects can be obtained in one-colour jobs, and the task of designing single-colour jobs comprises, as any typographer knows, the greater part of contemporary printing.

The kind of contrast required is decisive in the choice of a type mixture in publicity matter. A lively yet carefully chosen mixture is refreshing. *Gill* light with *Old Black*, for instance, is quite pleasing in its contrast between two types of different shape. Many contrasts have historical precedents, but we need not look for such a precedent in our type mixtures. *Old Black* and *Script*, or bold *Egyptian* and italic, when combined under certain conditions can work out in a thoroughly modern way.

All the type mixing possibilities considered apply equally to symmetrical or asymmetrical settings. Nevertheless there is a danger of 'traditionalism' in their use in centred layouts. In asymmetrical settings the danger of 'traditionalism' is far less great even for type mixtures with historical precedence.

In this supplement of new types are shown and reviewed five faces: below is Intertype *Egmont,* and in the succeeding pages are shown *City* (not new but not well known in this country) from the Berthold Typefoundry; *Offenbach,* one of Rudolf Koch's last designs, from Klingspor; *Slimblack* from Deberny et Peignot, Paris; and one new Monotype face

---

This is the twenty-four point size of Egmont, designed by S. H. de Roos, the Dutch artist and type designer. This type was originally cut for the Amsterdam Typefoundry, but is available in England through Intertype Limited. This is full alphabet ABCDEFGHIJKLMNOPQRST UVWXYZ abcdefghijklmnopqrstuvwxyz 1234567890 Egmont is available from the

eight point size. Very clear, very sharp, to the

The medium weight, this, is available from 8-point to the

24-POINT SIZE

24-POINT SIZE

ABCDEFGHIJKLMNOPQRSTUVWXYZ abcdefghijklmnopqrstuvwxyz

EGMONT: available in 8 10 12 14 18 24-point in light and medium, roman and italic matrices with true cut small caps: INTERTYPE LTD.

Those of our readers who know their private presses will recognize the hand of Mr. S. H. de Roos in this *Egmont* design. For those who are unacquainted with the work of the Dutch private presses, especially the *De Zilverdistel* and the more recent *De Heuvelpers,* we would add that Mr. de Roos was one of the first of the modern (modern in the

post-William Morris sense) designers of Dutch types. Specimens of his other type designs, *Dutch Mediæval* (1912), *Zilver* (1915), *Erasmus Mediæval* (1922), *Grotius* (1925) and *Meidoorn* (1927), will be found with full critical examination in *The Fleuron* No. VII.

The type under our consideration shows no radical departure from Mr. de Roos's earlier designs. There is the same highly individual decorative touch; the same skill and refinement in letter detail characteristic of the work

of this conscientious designer.

We have no idea of the precise intention of the designer as to how this face should be used and it is probable that Mr. de Roos makes no claim for *Egmont* as a book face. For booklet and advertisement typography this type is a handsome addition to any printer's repertoire and it can be especially recommended to Intertype users as a valuable addition to their display faces. We hope this will not be Intertype's only continental excursion. J. S.

typography must be modified historically when serving the reading habits of the twentieth century. I do not suggest that books should be printed as are newspapers, but I do suggest that reading habits and their relation to legibility are neither as conventional nor inflexible as the pure book typographer would have us believe.

Shand supplements his sociological arguments with technical ones, giving an extensive list of new developments which had changed, and would change, the face of printing – cylinder presses, pyramid ink rollers, an increased range of paper surfaces, 'bled' edges, steel stitching and spiral binding and of course the new printing processes: 'To the typographer offset lithography and rotary photogravure are no longer remote luxury processes but economical alternatives for large areas of flat colour, reversed line, composite text and illustration, on a variety of paper surfaces not possible for half-tone reproduction by letterpress printing.' Shand concludes that the 'shape of typography to come will be governed by an audience continually bombarded ·by newspapers, periodicals, propaganda and advertising, not to mention talking films'; as he puts it, 'an audience with a camera-eye'.

Harling's article is concerned with the rise of the pre-printed case as an alternative to expensive and fragile dust-jackets. He begins with the story of Victor Gollancz's success with the yellow dust-jacket and sparse typography in 1928 and how the idea was imitated and developed by, among others, Faber & Faber. In five years, under the direction of Richard de la Mare (the son of the poet), Faber reached a position where they were producing some of the finest books for their price in this country. Half the secret was that de la Mare was able to use the services of such artists as Edward Bawden and Barnett Freedman who were well acquainted with the practical limitations and potentialities of such a medium as offset lithography on pre-stamped cloth; very few artists had such knowledge. Of Richard de la Mare, Harling writes: 'He says, more than half seriously, that this appalling ignorance of methods of reproduction was the main reason for his prompting Harold Curwen to write his manual, *Processes of Graphic Reproduction in Printing*.' Harling finishes by giving some very encouraging advice to artists:

For a long, long time it has been the rule that the artist or designer who has been willing to experiment, walks off with some very desirable plums. From the Beggarstaff Brothers to Kauffer in the poster world, from Octavius Hill to Man Ray in the photographic world, from Wedgwood to Keith Murray in the pottery world, and so you can go on. There is now a new field waiting for the artist or designer who can spare the necessary time and has the necessary interest to explore and exploit the possibilities of the case.

Together with other articles on newspaper typography, two appreciations of the work of Stanley Morison, and some type specimens, this was the content of *Typography* No. 1. Though brief in all respects it was certainly 'stimulating and welcome'; it could wear the caps of pioneer and forum as *The Fleuron* could not. The contributions of Meynell, Shand and Harling were just what was needed at that time in that they were radical, challenging rather than outspoken, and confident.

Typography was received by the critics with enthusiasm. Issue No. 2 includes some letters from well-wishers – notably Eric Gregory, director of Lund Humphries, who published *Penrose's Annual* – and quotations from reviews. The *Times Literary Supplement* wrote: 'It has liveliness and learning, and a striking modern format which lends the weight of example to its words. It is not iconoclastic, but it examines old formulas in the light of today's needs.' Bernard Newdigate, in the *London Mercury*, confessed that he was 'bewildered by its make-up', finding it 'difficult to see the trees for the jungle of specimens, insets and advertisements', but concluded: 'When he (the reader) has winnowed the good grain from the chaff, he will find excellent value for his florin.' The reviewer in the *Architectural Review* wrote at length with high enthusiasm:

> . . . one can say at once that the first issue of *Typography*, presented in a cover of particular charm and distinction, maintains throughout the pages a standard of typesetting and design of the highest class; and one that is not afraid to be, in the best sense, modern – that is to say, to maintain a modern experimental spirit that is original in a constructive sense, not merely mannered.[4]

In issue No. 2 was a list of all the typefaces used in the number; all the text but that of one article was set in 10 on 12 point Monotype faces, namely Modern, Imprint, Plantin, Baskerville and Garamond. Harling added; '*Typography*'s purpose is to show, by example and experiment, the potentialities of existing material, used in publishing, printing and advertising.' The one article not using Monotype materials was 'Slug' by James Shand, set in Linotype Baskerville. While welcoming the variety of faces available, Shand confesses that he is worried about the manufacturers of matrices:

> . . . it is immediately evident that an immense influence on typography, and the future of typography, lies in the hands of these manufacturers of machines. Are they conscious of that responsibility? Is their policy, as makers of matrices, to interpret with historical judgement and typefounding skill, the larger requirements of the community in the designs they are making available to the printer? Are they conscious of the historical continuity of their role of twentieth-century typefounding and typesetting technicians?

39. (Overleaf)
Typography No. 3:
'Interpretative Typography Applied to School Geometry' by Peggy Laing.

THEOREM 27. (Pythagoras' Theorem.)

In any right-angled triangle, the square on the hypotenuse is equal to the sum of the squares on the sides containing the right angle.

Given ∠BAC is a right angle.

To prove the square on BC = the square on BA + the square on AC.

Let ABHK, ACMN, BCPQ be the squares on AB, AC, BC.

Join CH, AQ. Through A, draw AXY parallel to BQ, cutting BC, QP at X, Y.

Since ∠BAC and ∠BAK are right angles, KA and AC are in the same straight line.

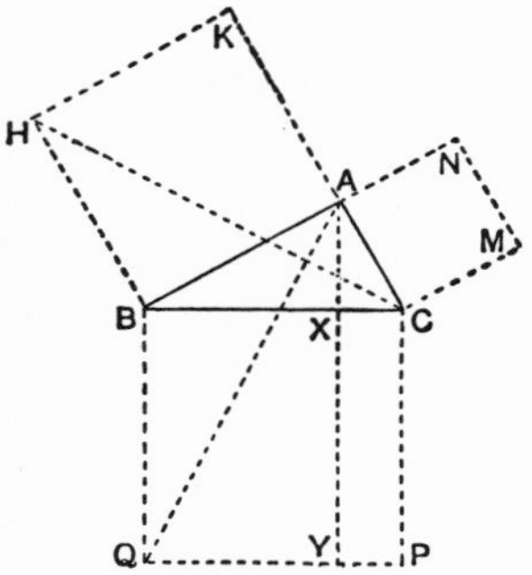

Again ∠HBA = 90° = ∠QBC.

Add to each ∠ABC, ∴ ∠HBC = ∠ABQ.

In the △s HBC, ABQ.

$$HB = AB, \text{ sides of square.}$$
$$CB = QB, \text{ sides of square.}$$
$$\angle HBC = \angle ABQ, \text{ proved.}$$
$$\therefore \triangle HBC \equiv \triangle ABQ \text{ (2 sides, inc. angle).}$$

Now △HBC and square HA are on the same base HB and between the same parallels HB, KAC ;

$$\therefore \triangle HBC = \tfrac{1}{2} \text{ square HA.}$$

Also △ABQ and rectangle BQYX are on the same base BQ and between the same parallels BQ, AXY.

$$\therefore \triangle ABQ = \tfrac{1}{2} \text{ rect. BQYX.}$$
$$\therefore \text{ square HA} = \text{rect. BQYX.}$$

Similarly, by joining AP, BM, it can be shown that square MA = rect. CPYX ;

$$\therefore \text{ square HA} + \text{square MA} = \text{rect. BQYX} + \text{rect. CPYX}$$
$$= \text{square BP.} \qquad \textbf{Q.E.D.}$$

Fig. 163.

Page from C. V. Durell's 'Elementary Geometry,' (G. Bell & Sons, Ltd., 1936).

and the number of the theorem probably means nothing to him. He merely needs to recognize the *Hypothesis*. If it is in bold type, it will jump to his eyes immediately.

The *Data* is just a statement of fact. If we print it thus :

Given: H, K are the middle points of **AB, AC**

and lead amply before we say :

To prove: HK is parallel to **BC** and **HK** = ½ **BC**

the two sections are easily distinguished.

Next comes the *Construction*. This tells the student *what to do*, not *what to think*. It is only the means of finding the proof, not part of the proof itself. It would seem reasonable therefore to set it in 262 italic, and lead again before beginning the *Proof* in roman upper- and lower-case. The accompanying layout of the Pythagoras theorem suggests a way of dealing with the *Proof* so that

THEOREM 27 (Pythogoras' Theorem)

In any right-angled triangle, the square on the hypotenuse is equal to the sum of the squares on the sides containing the right angle

Given: BAC is a right angle

To prove: the square on **BC**=

the square on **BA**+the square on **AC**

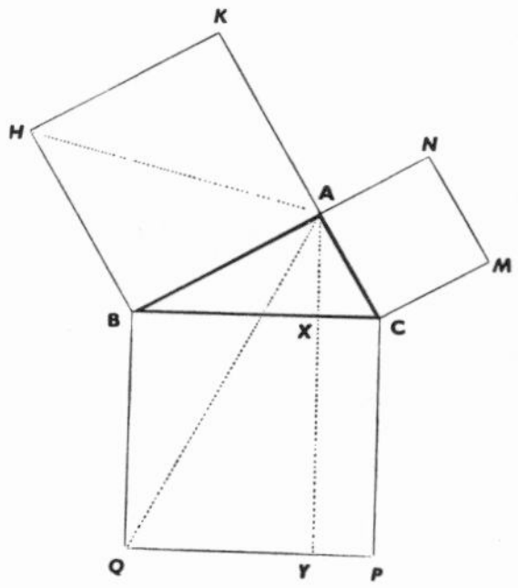

Let **ABHK, ACMN, BCPQ** be the squares on **AB, AC, BC**

Join **CH, AQ.** Through **A,** draw **AXY** parallel to **BQ,** cutting **BC, QP** at **XY**

Since BAC and BAK are rt. angles **KA** and **AC** are in the same str. line

Again *HBA*=90°=*QBC*
Add to each ABC
∴*HBC*=*ABQ*

In the △s **HBC, ABQ**
HB=**AB,** *sides of square*
CB=**QB,** ,, ,, ,,
HBC=*ABQ, proved*

Fig. 163

∴ △**HBC**= △**ABQ** (*2 sides, inc. angle*)

Now △**HBC** and square **HA** are on the same base **BQ** and between the same parallels **HB, KAC**

∴ △**HBC**= ½ square **HA**

Also △**ABQ** and rectangle **BQYX** are on the same base **BQ** and between the same parallels **BQ, AXY**

∴ △**ABQ**= ½ rect. **BQYX**
∴square **HA**= rect. **BQYX**

Similarly, *by joining* **AP, BM,** *it can be shown that*
square **MA**=rect. **CPYX**

∴square **HA**+square **MA**=rect. **BQYX**+rect. **CPYX**
=square **BP**

Q.E.D.

The same page re-designed in 9-point Gill Sans, Series 262 and 275.

the progress of the argument is easily followed.

If we agree that italic is to be used for the *Construction*, it will be logical to label the 'constructed' parts of the diagram with bold italic capitals, to distinguish them from the basic diagram with its roman 275 lettering.

In referring to angles, the arms could be named in 262, thus A**B**C, D**E**F, to distinguish from triangles symbolized as **ABC, DEF,** etc.

Although all contemporary school-geometry books are similar in content, their arrangement differs considerably, not only in the sequence of matter, but in the design of the pages. The study of various examples will suggest more difficulties to be overcome, and new ways of meeting others. The above suggestions are submitted as a mere basis for designing a workable text-book, intended to teach, among other things, the art of reasoning.

As Shand points out, the Monotype production programme was safe in the expert hands of Stanley Morison, and this article was concerned solely with slug typography, that is to say Linotype and to a lesser extent Intertype and Ludlow. He points out that, as slug casting arrived before single type, its manufacturers and admirers had a hard job getting the equipment installed where hand-compositors were once used to doing all the setting in the house. 'The slug had to prove the virtues, advantages and possibilities for the radical innovation of simultaneous casting and composing.' Although slug casting had been confined largely to newspapers and periodicals, Shand provides tipped-in examples from four book printers, including a Nonesuch title page set in Estienne, and an illustrated opening from the Cresset Press superbly set in Granjon. These examples prove Shand's claim that good slug-composition can fulfil the most stringent requirements of set, spacing and accuracy of casting both in design and type height. The author goes on to praise the production programmes of Linotype, Intertype and Ludlow which were making available to the printer the finest of faces, ancient and modern, though he is sorry that there are gaps: 'Is it too pious to speculate on an interchange of new designs [between Mono and Lino] and on the subsidising and organising of a definitive examination of original sources?'

The best early issue of *Typography* was surely No. 3. The opening article is written by Jan Tschichold and is entitled 'Type Mixtures'. While the practice of mixing type to achieve emphasis has been propagated since the time of Gutenberg, it was never more abused than in the Victorian era: 'In 1870, for example, it was considered good-class work to set the names of twenty different products on a letter-heading in twenty different typefaces of the same body size, producing a lamentable lack of typographic discipline and complete confusion.' The word 'discipline' shows clearly that the author of the article was Tschichold. His contribution was translated from the German by Ellic Howe.

Tschichold goes on to say that the concept of type harmony was first used by William Morris and that the idea has been developed ever since. He lays down rules: type mixing within the text of a book should be confined to the use of italics, bold and small capitals of the text face. His rules regarding display matter are more easily explained by the use of his illustrations. He concludes: 'All the type mixing possibilities considered apply equally to symmetrical or asymmetrical settings. Nevertheless there is a danger of "traditionalism" in their use in centred layouts. In asymmetrical settings the danger of "traditionalism" is far less great even for type mixtures with historical precedence.' For Tschichold this article was a good opportunity to set down some of the principles of functional typography before an English audience; for Harling, the contribution was something of a triumph – Tschichold's ideas were just beginning to take root in England at this time, for example at the Double Crown Club where Tschichold was invited to speak at their fortieth dinner in 1937.

40. *Typography* No. 4: 'The Optical Scale of Typefounding' by Harry Carter.

size; moreover, by modern standards we should hardly judge his 14-point and his 18-point to be members of one family.

It is worth considering whether the modern type-producers ought not to allow themselves more latitude in adapting a general design for a face to the various bodies on which they put it. Now that punches are cut under industrial conditions by a mechanical process it is easy to make the various sizes perfectly uniform—easier, in fact, than to differentiate them. A hand-punchcutter would have had to be extremely skilful to reproduce precisely the same letters on a dozen different scales. It is clear to anyone who can examine enlargements of hand-cut types that the good punchcutters varied the design, or at any rate the functional features of it, to suit the scale on which they worked. They did so instinctively because they corrected their work by eye, and they had the wisdom not to let mathematical rules override their judgment. The modern process of type-production, being departmentalized, lacks the advantage of being controlled during its progress by one expert eye. One man draws the type, another cuts it; corrections can only be made by scrapping valuable work. Because of the additional labour and time involved in making drawings for each size of type, and separate sets of patterns for the cutter to follow, differentiations between sizes are kept down to a minimum in modern typefounding.

There are some types, sanserifs particularly, that are patient of rule-of-thumb enlargement and diminution; it is the calligraphic types that need carefully adapting for various sizes. During the last twenty years industrial type-production has learned a good deal from the old masters of punch-cutting. The majority of present-day book-founts are modelled on hand-cut originals belonging to an earlier age, and the study of old types has certainly improved the typefounder's technique. The types of twenty-five years ago were too much influenced by the facility of the pantographic drill, which can cut the Lord's Prayer in relief on a $\frac{1}{6}$-inch square. When the machine first came into use the tendency was to show off its marvellous precision: later on, people realized that the pantography, with all its advantages of speed and low labour-cost, could do nothing worth while that a hand-cutter could not do.

A type-design is usually judged by its suitability for a page of an octavo book, and so the 11- to 14-point sizes are the most critically examined. I think it is true to say that text-types stand or fall by the technical skill of their execution rather than by the beauty of their design. Lack of interest in the design only becomes a serious objection when the type is drawn for a body of 16-point or more.

For many centuries Caslon's pica has been a favourite, and yet as a piece of drawing it is relatively dull. It has

Above: 9-point Modern Extended—the type used until lately for 'The Times.' A very fine engineer's job, but a poor design for reproduction on so small a scale

The 6-point and 10-point hand-cut by Walbaum. The relatively low join in the n and bolder serifs in the smaller size are good features

In the same issue is an article on 'Left-Wing Layout', by Howard Wadman. Wadman says that there are two kinds of socialist typography:

First there is the Clinical or Timetable school of layout. This is an affair of graduated rules, sans serif and chilly wastes of white. It came out of constructivism and the mechanic passion of the first five-year plan, when on the Moscow stage even *Hamlet* called for girders and three-dimensional geometry. Lissitzky and Tschichold are, of course, the masters of Clinical typography . . . The second main style . . . is what one may call the Proletarian (or Damn-your-eyes) School. It is a product of the increasing tension in world affairs. Heavy Egyptian letters, crude photomontage, coloured cut-outs heavily overprinted in black, and brutal charcoal drawings give to this type of propaganda terrific power of visual assault. By some curious twist, bad printing becomes a virtue, and ragged edges, faulty register and filled half-tones are all part of the picture.

Unfortunately, Wadman does not attempt to link these two widely differing styles in any way, to show that they have grown out of a united school of thought. He does suggest that neither fulfils its purpose:

I incline to the view that the masses cannot be either intellectualized or blasted into a Left position. Left-wing ideas must be *sold* to them as Mr Gollancz sells his books, namely by treating them like normal merchandise, and giving them the carefully planned, lively but dispassionate sales promotion which is enjoyed by a crustless cheese or a cure for constipation. . . . Gollancz has shaken the genteel flummery out of publishing and made it a business. Left-wing propaganda has to go the same way.

Among the other valuable contributions to issue No. 3 is one by Frederic Goudy on 'Ampersands'. The article is a history of the ampersand from the first century B C and is illustrated with seventy-eight examples, all drawn by the author: only in the fifteenth century does the symbol take on a form consistently recognisable to the modern eye. Goudy emphasises its construction: '. . . an ampersand is not a cipher, as some writers have called it; it is instead a true monogram in which *one* character signifies the two letters that compose it [e and t].' In designing ampersands for founts of his own design (several of which are illustrated), Goudy claims that he has invariably 'undertaken to make a character which would suggest *et* and be also in complete harmony with the letters of the fount.' Goudy also announces that he has designed one hundred typefaces at the time of writing.

Two other contributions to issue No. 3 deserve special mention; Ellic Howe writes on illustration processes in the nineteenth century in 'From Bewick to the Half-tone', and there is also a contribution from Peggy Laing in a practical and

41. *Typography* No. 4: 'Handwriting Reform' by Alfred Fairbank. Set in Monotype Narrow Bembo.

and an angle of 45° to 50° of the hair–line to the writing line will give letters the elegance of height.

The illustrations to this article have been chosen principally to give some inkling of the various excellencies of XVI–century italic scripts, but also because collectively they will suffice as models. For those who would wish however to have a precise contemporary model, shorn of archaisms, and related to rather than strictly imitative of XVI–century hands, reference may perhaps be permitted to the author's 'Handwriting Manual' and 'Barking Writing Cards'.★

The first letters that the reformer should learn and practise are n, m, u, and a. The following word would not be acceptable to a printer: *auuouuce*. And yet something equivalent will commonly be found in contemporary handwriting for the word 'announce'. For legibility an 'n' must be an 'n' and not a 'u'. Both legibility and speed are linked up with the problem of making 'n' and 'u' distinct, for the success or failure will depend upon the rhythm of writing. To write quickly is to write with a certain rhythm. The rhythm may be conditioned by the proper shapes of letters and meet the needs of both legibility and speed. Figure 5 is of writing by a XVI–century penman and shows an understanding of this particular problem of rhythm and legibility.

Joins, connecting letters together, help one to write quickly and rhythmically, but that is not to argue that all letters should therefore be joined. Pen–lifts, if not very frequent, also serve the hand and script. The happy mean is between the two extremes of lifting the pen after every letter and lifting the pen only when the last letter of the word is written. The diagonal join is an upstroke and therefore is best made by a sideways movement of the pen. The horizontal join connects the tops of certain letters: e.g., as from an 'o' to an 'n'.

For capitals reference may well be made to Gill Sanserif italic ABCDEFGHIJKLMNOPQRSTUVWXYZ or to the freer swash capitals in the alphabets shown in figure 6, and a discerning discretion exercised. The whole reform of a hand-writing may begin suitably by experiments with capitals: by tentative immersions of the feet before a decisive plunge.

No excuse is necessary for again quoting the late W. R. Lethaby: 'Common interest in the improvement of ordinary writing would be an immense disciplinary force: we might reform the world if we began with our own handwriting, but we certainly shall not unless we begin somewhere'.

★ Dryad Press, Leicester.

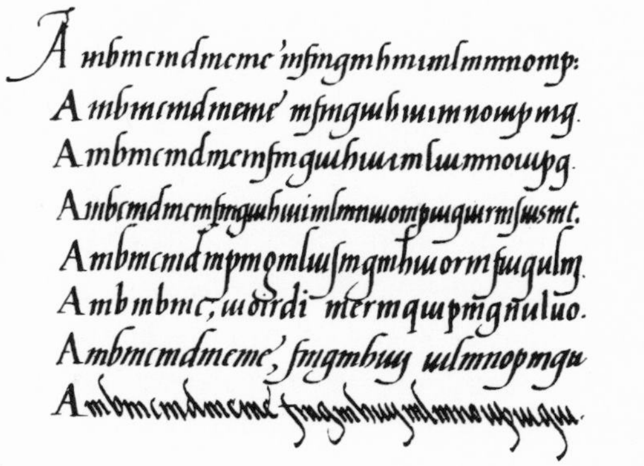

Fig. 5. From an album of alphabets. British Museum (Add. 27869). Slightly reduced

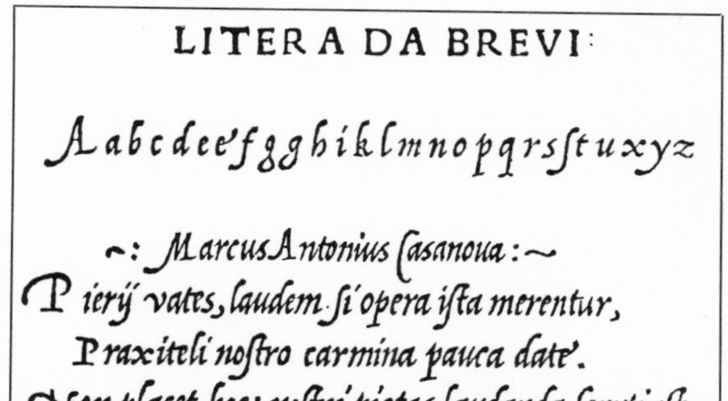

Fig. 6. From the writing–book of Ludovico Vicentino, 'Il modo de temperare le penne'. Venice, 1523

well-illustrated article called 'Interpretative Typography Applied to School Geometry'. Howe's article, probably the longest to appear in the pages of *Typography*, is a comprehensive and learned approach to the subject well worth close examination. Peggy Laing's is another example of the contemporary outlook that Harling was so keen to embody; the article outlines new methods of laying out geometry text books and the design of geometric symbols.

The contents of issue No. 4 could hardly have equalled those of No. 3. The opening article is written by Harry Carter and concerns 'The Optical Scale in Typefounding'; it compares various body sizes of one typeface, indicating and explaining the dissimilarities, the reason usually being legibility. Misha Black, the industrial designer, writes on dust wrappers, making a strong plea for more original and up-to-date thought on the subject. Perhaps the best article is 'Handwriting Reform' by Alfred Fairbank; it is beautifully set in Fairbank's Monotype Narrow Bembo (Series 294) and is, of course, concerned with calligraphy and its influence on type design.

In the introductory notes, Harling wrote:

With this issue *Typography* comes to the end of its first year. The history of that year has been a success story, however modest. First, the economics of the venture have been far less onerous than anticipated. Second, circulation figures improve monthly. Indeed we doubt whether any other quarterly, with the exception of *The Countryman*, has ever grown at such a satisfying rate. Third, these figures will continue to grow.

Harling acknowledges that a certain amount of the financial success is due to the advertising which *Typography* took from the printing trade, but he seems confident that his journal has been received with respect and pleasure.

Issue No. 5 begins with an editorial statement of the journal's new production policy: 'We shall not offer so many mounted inserts, but propose to include more colour in the body of the book, thus offering a greater unity in the journal, a greater sense of continuity in content.'

The opening article, by Eric Gill, although entitled 'The Work of Denis Tegetmeier', is more a thesis on the role of the artist in society – 'the artist is first of all a workman; a servant. He does not exist simply to tickle his own fancy.' Gill is referring to the artist as an illustrator, who 'is not showing off or airing his idiosyncrasy; he is doing a job of work in harmony with printers and writers.' One is reminded sharply of the relationship between the craftsmen at Curwen and the artists brought in by Oliver Simon and Harold Curwen. Gill, himself an artist of considerable skill and vision, is generous in his praise of Tegetmeier; 'Tegetmeier's drawings are things, and imitations of things. They are not translations. They are creations; for what he draws has no other mode of existence.' Illustrations are reproduced from *The Seven Deadly Virtues* and Gill's own *Money and Morals*.

42. *Typography* No. 5: 'Timetable Typography' by Christian Barman.

10 Genève-Lausanne-Fribourg-Bern (-Basel u. Zürich)   Traction électrique

Fig. 7. Page from Swiss Amtliches Kursbuch showing use of extra condensed and sans italic

57 p (124 c) Glatz—Waldenburg-Dittersbach
Alle Züge 2. u. 3. Kl.

58 (153) Halle (Saale)—[Leipzig—] Cottbus—Sagan
Alle Züge, soweit nicht anders vermerkt, 2. u. 3. Kl.

Fig. 8. Section from the German Reichs Kursbuch which is, claims Mr. Barman, the most complete, the best edited and the best printed timetable in the world. A model of how these things should be done

The major article in issue No. 5 is Christian Barman's 'Timetable Typography'. Barman was then in charge of publicity for London Transport and so was perhaps uniquely qualified to write the history of 100 years of timetables and to examine the virtues and defects of modern timetable design. He outlines the career of Bradshaw's timetables, and shows that their design hardly changed for a century. As travel became more extensive and more complicated, so the problems in timetable design became more difficult to solve. The use of symbols was highly desirable and setting in sans serif faces became general. Lines were often set along a column, requiring the turning of a page. The disposition of weights and condensed faces was of critical importance. Barman investigates closely the decision in 1933 of the London Passenger Transport Board to give up sans serif in favour of Times New Roman as recommended by Francis Meynell. Each character and numeral was to be as distinctive as possible without being caricatured. Long runs on cheap paper in 'rush' conditions made this essential. Figures were to be presented in two weights (for a.m. and p.m.); this could be done as effectively but with more subtlety if thick and thin strokes were used. Thirdly, serifs facilitated the reading of a line. A further innovation was contributed by Harold Curwen, namely the presentation of type in blocks of five lines each, helping the user to follow a line and then to return to the beginning of the next without faltering. Thus, as Barman makes clear, the design of the timetable had returned to the simplicity of Bradshaw's, printed one hundred years earlier. 'The subject of a really good timetable is an exciting and complicated story. But whether you take the simplest or the most complicated, they all represent to the typographer just the same kind of fundamental problems that leave no loopholes for art or humour or any kind of escape.'

'Patent Medicine Advertising' (PMA) is the title of an article by Denis Butlin, an advertisement copywriter, which shows that PMA is deliberately out of date. After recalling the sneering attitude of a typographer whose loyalty was to the private press rather than to the 'hard sell' world of advertising, Butlin claims: 'Advertising is not intended as a method of cultural education although quite incidentally and despite itself it has been known to serve that purpose.' He suggests that PMA has to be old-fashioned for two very good reasons: (1) it is primarily aimed at the over-forties, who look to the remedies of their youth for relief from suffering, and (2) people tend to trust a product that has been advertised regularly for years; if the advertisement has not changed, then it (and the product itself) is sufficient and proven.

One of the hallmarks of *Typography* was the presence of articles written in this commercial vein, especially on the subject of advertising. In the years before the war Robert Harling was art director of a leading London advertising agency. At this period advertising was beginning to acquire the 'cut-throat' reputation that it carries today whilst seeking to suggest that it was becoming more responsible and more respectable, and Harling undoubtedly found in *Typography* a therapeutic

43. *Typography* No. 5: 'Patent Medicine Advertising' by Denis Butlin.

"I take no chances with CHILBLAINS"

says a schoolmistress

" I myself have always been susceptible to chilblains, and as soon as winter came in I would find that several of my girls had them also. I mentioned this to our new games mistress, and on her advice I started taking Calsimil tablets every day. I also gave some to girls who were 'chilblain subjects'. We all kept on with Calsimil, and there wasn't a chilblain in the whole form. Since then I've never waited for the first warning twinges of chilblains — I forestall the trouble by starting on Calsimil as soon as the colder weather sets in."

An important cause of chilblains is calcium deficiency. Calsimil, which contains Vitamin D, is calcium in its most easily absorbed form, for *only when Vitamin D is present can calcium be assimilated.* Begin *now* to take Calsimil—3 tablets a day. There is no surer protection against chilblains.

CALSIMIL
for chilblains

Calsimil brand Tablets from all chemists
— 2/6 for 60 tablets.

THE BRITISH DRUG HOUSES LTD. LONDON

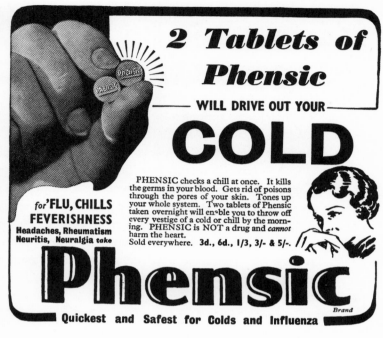

for 'FLU, CHILLS FEVERISHNESS
Headaches, Rheumatism Neuritis, Neuralgia take

2 Tablets of Phensic
WILL DRIVE OUT YOUR
COLD

PHENSIC checks a chill at once. It kills the germs in your blood. Gets rid of poisons through the pores of your skin. Tones up your whole system. Two tablets of Phensic taken overnight will enable you to throw off every vestige of a cold or chill by the morning. PHENSIC is NOT a drug and *cannot* harm the heart.
Sold everywhere. 3d., 6d., 1/3, 3/- & 5/-.

Phensic
Brand

Quickest and Safest for Colds and Influenza

Above: Real P M A stuff, even to the pointing hand!
Sound appeal to the 'B' and 'C' class markets
and unlikely to be missed in any newspaper
Ultra Bodoni italic makes its appearance, an unusual
touch in P M A typography

Left: An effort in a more sober direction. Condensed Sans,
Plantin 110, Bodoni italic and a touch of Times Roman
A generous mixture, but all quite sedate
The authentic touch retained with the reverse nameplate

---

bottle and by never changing brought stability to the product as only repetition can. To change now would be suicidal unless the advertiser were prepared to increase his appropriation, change his pack and splash a strong story of an 'improved product' in every medium in the land. Even then he would probably lose ground, and in any case such a hazardous piece of largess would require a better justification than the plea of 'catching up with the times'.

However, where a product is not so firmly established and its advertising not so well known, I see little reason why the advertising should not be tuned to the younger generation. But here again lie difficulties. One must heed another factor—the cultural time-lag that exists between the Metropolitan and the Provincial. Would ten years be too much? I doubt it. Whatever it is, it should be allowed for. And, of course, the copywriter, layout man and typographer must always allow an additional margin for the colossal time lag

that exists between his own mind and the mind of the reader. An unpleasant thought, a presumptuous thought perhaps, but true, I feel.

But from behind the black cloud I have sketched, sunshine is breaking—rather shyly, but it's coming. By my side is a small 6″ single column Calsimil advertisement with Condensed Sans used effectively in display and the ubiquitous *Plantin* 110 for the text. Also a Phyllosan effort utilizing *Caslon Heavy* in a reassuringly heavy manner, *Plantin* 110, and an interesting, well-posed photograph. I mention these because they are both well tuned to their 'B' class-minded, if not actually 'B' class, public.

In conclusion, my prizes for layout and *typographical judgment* go to Fynnon Salts as an example of Class 'C' appeal in the old-fashioned style; Dinneford's for Class 'C' appeal in 'modern' style, and Phensic for what it is—which is obvious.

escape from the more frenetic world of advertising. His efforts to improve and polish *Typography* are obvious to the reader and were occasionally viewed with some trepidition by Shand and his colleagues at the Shenval Press. Harling once suggested to Shand that he should travel to Hertford and look round the works, but Shand begged him not to, fearing that he might then ask them to do things they *could* do![5]

Issue No. 6 lacks the substance of its predecessor but contains some interesting articles. S. L. Righyni examines the typography of the provincial press, citing the *Scotsman* and the *Manchester Guardian* as two particularly well-designed and carefully produced provincial newspapers. The article was sparked off by the passing, as a daily, of the *Yorkshire Post*, thus reducing the number of provincial dailies to twenty-seven. As far as the typography of these papers is concerned, the author points out that the character of the provincial morning newspaper is generally one that appeals to a select circulation as against the mass appeals of the evening and national papers. The design and make-up of each has remained largely unchanged for many years. The finished product is never as highly developed as the national paper; 'It may have good sections but they are not carried out over the whole of the paper.'

Some biographical notes by Imre Reiner are followed by 'Notes on Some Seventeenth-Century English Types' by A. F. Johnson. He demonstrates that the trade in types was largely international and that the types were very durable.

> It may be supposed that English printers of the generation of Moxon bought their foreign types in the Netherlands but these types were by no means always cut by the founders who supplied them. The original punches may have been engraved in France or even in Italy, and, as likely as not, they may date from the middle years of the sixteenth century.[6]

This authoritative article is illustrated from, and makes frequent reference to, the Bagford collection of specimens and fragments in the British Museum, many items of which were previously unpublished.

John Betjeman chose to write on ecclesiastical typography, presenting 'the substance of a paper read with the invaluable aid of an epidiascope, to the Double Crown Club'.[7] He finishes by condemning the paper for being too superficial. 'Follow my advice; take a walk down Paternoster or Protestant (despite Sheed and Ward) Row or Square and *search the scriptures*.'

Betjeman's was the last *Typography* article to be treated with an individual design. For the last two numbers (and indeed for Harling's post-war journals) the design was made uniform throughout, reverting to what Harling termed 'typographical respectability'. Issue No. 7 was set throughout in Times Roman and Times Roman Bold. The first article to be treated thus was one of three major

44. *Typography* No. 6: 'Ecclesiastical Typography' by John Betjeman.

John Betjeman

HERE WRITES UPON THE SUBJECT OF

ECCLESIASTICAL TYPOGRAPHY

AND INSISTS UPON HIS APOLOGIA

(SEE CONTENTS PAGE)

THAT THIS IS A LIGHT PAPER, HAVING NO DEPTH

EXCEPT THAT BETWEEN HIGH AND LOW

★

IF THE PROSE STYLE of my article is a trifle florid in these, its initial stages, you will, I trust, forgive that floridity and blame it on the book which I was reading all day before I could bring myself to summon the courage to take up the pen and point it ready to commit to paper the words which sooner or later I knew must be forced out of my head on the subject of *Ecclesiastical Typography*. That book was Britton's *Autobiography*. Not Thomas Britton, 'the musical small coal man', but that John Britton, the antiquary, whose works on the *Beauties of England and Wales* (illustrated with Le Keux's steel engravings), whose *Beauties of Wiltshire*, whose song books, memorials, testimonials, etc., cover the years 1790-odd to 1850 and still fill the folio shelves of many a provincial bookshop. His autobiography covers that period on which my mind most delights to dwell—the late eighteenth and the first two decades of the early nineteenth century. Turning over its magic pages the eye is enchanted by the sight of many a great and now forgotten name in the literary, artistic, dramatic, typographical and topographical world, in caps. and s. caps. Not a page is dull, not a page badly proportioned. There are few misprints, and as I read on, fascinated by the antiquarian's narrative gift, what a flutter of playbills in *Albion, Elephant, Bell* filed through my subconscious mind! What a spread of copper and steel engraved title pages, of woodcuts of Stratford-on-Avon, of aquatints of coaches, of early lithographs of decaying castles, floated before my eyes! What panoramas, dioramas, kaleidoscopes, transformations, magic lanthorns, cameræ-obscuræ, patent eidaphusika, globes, transparencies, protean views, curiosa, miscellanea, and panoptica danced in many coloured confusion, shifting, changing colour like the big moments in the Lyceum Pantomime, crashing with mimic

thunder, spouting genuine New River water from the floorboards of Sadler's Wells to pre-Wagnerian romantic music! What gas lights jetted argent flame on snow scenes!

I hope, before this paper is ended, to have shaken off some of the fetters of this elaborate prose style. But I hope never to shake off the remembrance of that glorious age when Britain was still fit for the pencil of a Rowlandson, the pen of a Sir Walter and the voice of a Catalini, when London was the most beautiful capital in Europe, when books and printing were bright with the names of the Whittinghams and Pickering; when Jones's (late Lackington's) Temple of the Muses startled the world from Finsbury Square. An age before we had our eyesight blurred by the blackened pages of a Kelmscott book, before our sense of paper, binding and type had been affronted by string-encumbered paper and nail file binding, before our intelligence had been insulted by sexy dust covers and our sense of colour outraged by the productions of high-powered publishers.

These are hard things to write, gentlemen, so it is with pleasure and relief that I turn to my theme—Ecclesiastical Typography.

In religious publications we can still find traces of the early nineteenth century which produced that masterpiece of legible and shapely make-up, *Bradshaw's Guide*. And where there have been deviations from the old tradition, they are obvious and easy to trace—symptomatic of the age; though perhaps twenty years late. The churches, we are told, 'do not keep up with the times', and thank goodness they don't. There is a profound truth in their static positions which will, I seriously trust and believe never move them.

And here I must make a parenthesis. There is a great risk

articles concerned with aspects of contemporary print design, namely 'The Dictatorship of the Lay-out Man' by Holbrook Jackson. He begins:

> It is supposed that the character of the modern periodical has been determined by popular education, and to some extent that may be true. But it does not explain why most readers of periodical 'literature' prefer snippets and blurbs to full-length articles, and pictures to either.

Jackson unearths one of the ills of modern society as a possible reason: 'there is a large public, male and female, who resents mental effort of any kind.' This symptom, coupled with the invention of process engraving, had led to the pre-eminence of the illustrated periodical: 'It is no longer the editorial copy that counts, but its presentation.' And it seems that this was more true of this country than of any other. The reason behind this typographical disintegration was, of course, circulation figures; both publishing magnate and advertiser were keen to increase circulation. The advertiser, however, became dubious. 'Banner headlines, blurbs, text staggered by pictures are no longer clever; they are admissions of defeat. They say to readers: Abandon hope all ye who enter here.' Things were better in the United States but the damage here was far-reaching. 'The dictatorship of the lay-out man not only destroys readers – it destroys editors and writers.' Much work needed to be done to match the new American magazines *Time*, *Ken* and *Reader's Digest* (which used to carry no advertisements). The Americans had outclassed Britain – and were making it pay.

The second article, 'Visual Expression' by Ashley Havinden, is a thoughtful collection of notes written by one of the world's foremost advertisement and poster design artists. The subject is advertising design and the modern designer's approach to it. From a historical point of view, William Morris is blamed for preventing the emergence of a new aesthetic: as printing technology progressed he advocated archaic design as the only way of preserving any semblance of culture in the machine age. 'I think we all recognize today that new forms, and indeed new standards, are needed if we are to adapt ourselves to the changed conditions of today.' After demonstrating the incompatibility of outdated concepts and modern needs, Havinden outlines the considerations of the advertising designer – firstly the copywriter, then the audience and the immediate circumstances of that audience. He demonstrates the inherent danger of applying preconceived ideas to any design, concluding that '. . . in the course of trying to solve these problems he tends to get too preoccupied with the artistic possibilities of his work at the expense of its clarity.' Havinden's creed can be summed up in his own words: 'I believe that the only ideal a designer should work to is complete clarity of expression.' He rejects modern 'cubist' design except in its application to modern images, thus proving his original thesis: 'I am convinced that, through the inventive skill of scientists and

45. *Typography* No. 7: 'Visual Expression' by Ashley Havinden.

46. (Overleaf, left) *Typography* No. 7: 'Early Children's ABC's' by Roland Knaster.

47. (Overleaf, right) *Typography* No. 7: 'Twentieth-Century Sans Serifs' by Denis Megaw.

EXHIBITION OF PICTURES IN ADVERTISING BY SHELL-MEX AND B.P. LTD.

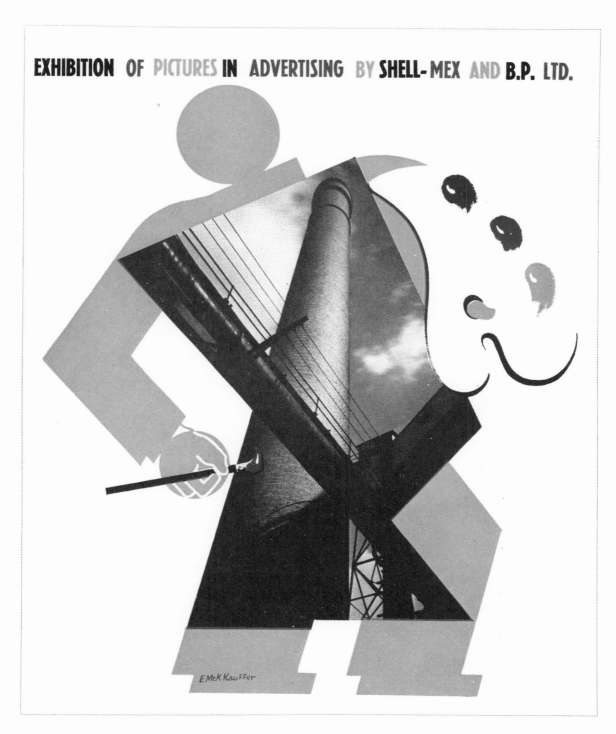

E McK Kauffer

'The great work of McKnight Kauffer alone is proof of the forcefulness of modern forms when handled by a master designer'

Double-page spread of an ABC published by A. Ryle, successor to J. Catnach. Circa 1840

delightful ABC's were printed abroad, but mention can only be made of two. Lefuel, of Paris, published *circa* 1820 a magnificent ABC: *ABÈCÈDAIRE des Petits Gourmands rédigé par Mma Dufrenoy*, with a most delicately lithographed ABC by Constans from drawings by Develly (C—Cerises, O—Omelette). About 1835, Langlumé, of Paris, published a coloured panoramic ABC in which all the Professions and Trades were illustrated by Animals: A—Avocat (Parrot); C—Chanteur (Cat) and I—Imprimeur (Monkey), and below the latter is inscribed, 'M. Lesinge compositeur d'imprimerie en extase devant son travail'.

The ABC's included in section 'c' are another treasure-trove for all who care for beauty of production and ingenuity of type. The historic ABC of this section is undoubtedly William Jole's *A little Book for little Children*, published *circa* 1708, and which contained the immortal, 'A was an Archer and Shot at a Frog', ending, not with the inevitable 'Z was a Zebra . . .', but with 'Z was one Zeno the Great, but he's dead'. Between this date and the early nineteenth century the few ABC's that were printed, other than Hornbooks and Battledores, were mostly of the Chapbook type; a few being bound in Dutch flowered-paper, the result being as fine a specimen of book-production, as any to be seen to-day.

One example of this type was printed by Poole, of Taunton (*circa* 1790):

Poetical emblems, suited to each Letter of the

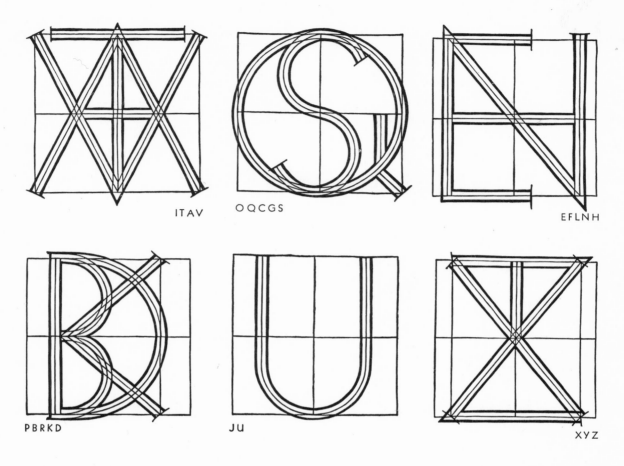

ITAV   OQCGS   EFLNH

PBRKD   JU   XYZ

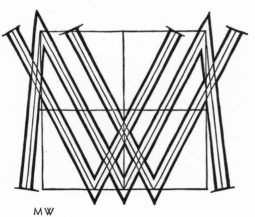

MW

The following notes are taken from a prospectus produced for the Cable type:

Roman caps are the basic forms of classical lower-case as well as of all the Nordic and German characters. They have their roots in the highest peak of Roman rule, and are the simplest form of letter. These sleek signs are made up of very few geometric forms: |O o

From a straight line at various angles; from a large and small circle, or sectors of them, all the letters of roman type are composed...

A remarkable variety of letter widths is produced by the succession of letters thus constructed. Narrow, wide and medium forms alternate in irregular order. This alternation produces lively movement, which is stimulating and refreshing to the reader. At all times this play of form and width has been understood; only in the last generation did type-designers think of replacing this variation by regularity.

Almost all of our 'grotesque' types hitherto have this deadness of set and monotonous effect which render them unsuitable for most present-day uses.

The illustrated constructional drawings divide the letters into seven kinds, all of which are based on the square. By the conjoining the construction is made understandable, and, above all, the varying widths of the letters defined and justified.

THE BASIC SHAPES OF THE CABLE SANS SERIF DESIGNED BY RUDOLF KOCH

engineers, collaborating with the designer, a new world of visual pleasure is grow-
ing up around us.'

The third major article is a review of 'Twentieth-Century Sans Serif Types' by
Denis Megaw. After a brief look at the Victorian display faces, Megaw sees the
origin of Johnston's sans in the designs of the *Jugendstil* (Nonage style) letterers of
Germany. If the essential difference between English and German sans serifs is that
English design finds its roots in the humanistic letters of fifteenth-century scribes
while German design is geometrical ('mechanistic') – though both derive ulti-
mately from the Trajan capitals – the rationality of Johnston's design surely indi-
cates the presence of German precedents. Reproduced as an illustration is Johnston's
argument for his original design. His limit of weight was defined firstly by the
effect of weight on transversely divided capitals (A, B, E, etc.) and secondly by the
need to match a lower-case to its upper-case. Johnston's limit of weight was one
fifth of the height of the capitals. In Gill's sans serif design, Megaw sees little improvement on Johnston's, though he admits that the face has innate qualities: 'The
Monotype Corporation undoubtedly showed a profound commercial wisdom in
introducing a sans in which the typographical intelligentsia might find their beloved
aesthetics and in which workaday printers could find no pyrotechnics.' The third
indigenous design is Harold Curwen's, which follows Johnston's, 'though not so
closely as to preclude all originality'. Megaw concludes that these and 'a score of
more or lesser-known designs . . . form the most powerful and ubiquitous set of
type forms in the world of printing.' However, he plays down their importance
in favour of those who are to use them: 'Sans has no more special significance for
the twentieth century than twentieth-century typographers are capable of demonstrating.'

Other articles in issue No. 7 include Roland Knaster's 'Early Children's ABC's'
and John Carter's 'The Typography of the Cheap Reprint Series'. Stephenson
Blake's Playbill is among the type reviews, while James Shand reviews, among
other titles, the second edition of Updike's *Printing Types*, Newdigate's *The Art of
the Book* and Holbrook Jackson's *The Printing of Books*. And, as Harling comments,
'There are the usual notes and comments on the typographical world or things
which seem even remotely related to the typographical world.' Harling philo-
sophically called *Typography* 'a spare-time job', although it is doubtful if the
returns could have justified the volume of work involved. It is worth quoting at
length from Harling's last *Typography* editorial, for he indulges in a little self-
analysis:

> Both publisher and editor, as you may know, are reasonably busy men with
> fairly full days. One has been called a 'highbrow publisher, commercial printer',
> the other is an advertising agency art director. That means that *Typography* is
> literally a spare-time job. We started the venture with the idea of keeping to
> quarterly publishing dates, but it seems that this was a somewhat optimistic

48. *Typography* No. 8:
'Lament for a Bluebook
Bureaucracy'
by R. S. Hutchings.

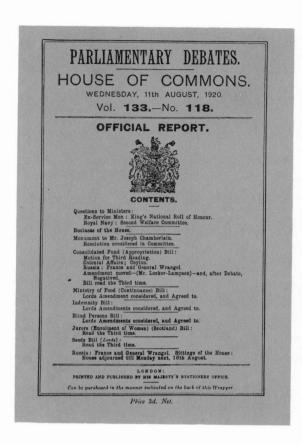

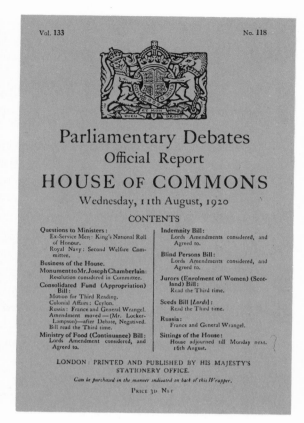

The typographical progress of Hansard: (i) 1920 version (ii) 1922 Committee's suggested restyling

especially necessary to have regard to the cost of production. At the same time good printing is, within limits, by no means inconsistent with economy. To set work in type of good design costs no more than to set it in type of poor design; and in any case there is no reason why the price of any Government publication issued for sale upon a commercial basis should not be so calculated as to cover the full cost of production.'

'There can be little doubt,' the Report continued, 'that a well-printed book is not only more legible, but also more saleable than a book that is ill-printed; and on general grounds Government printing in a country which can claim so many of the great printers of the past ought to be as good as possible consistent with economy. The Government should set the highest standard practicable in the various classes of its own productions and so help to improve the public taste . . . In this connexion it will not be out of place to refer to the great influence exercised in the closing years

of the last century by some of the State printing presses on the Continent. The fine quality of work which they issued undoubtedly helped to raise the standard of production of the commercial presses of their respective countries; and the Committee submit that, without embarking upon any policy so ambitious as this, the Government is in a position to exercise a great influence for good upon the printing craft, partly by achieving a high standard in its own work and partly by requiring the same high standard in work put out to contract.'

The examples of text types shown in the Report included *Monotype Imprint, Plantin* 110, *Caslon, and Scotch; Linotype Bodoni, Bodoni Book, and Scotch;* and hand-set types from the Caslon, Stephenson & Blake, Shanks, and Miller & Richard foundries. In the layout section, eight wrappers of existing Stationery Office publications were shown facing the restyled settings recommended by the Committee and followed by their respective title-pages; while two pages were

calculation. Yet, defiantly, we shall continue to call ourselves a 'quarterly'. We like the word – it's so pleasantly academic and unlike ourselves, and you will still get four issues for your so-called annual subscription. When you see that word 'quarterly' we suggest you smile sardonically (or understandingly, dependent on your temperament, of course) and carefully refrain from looking at the seasons we have omitted in our progress from first proof to publication day.

The articles in issue No. 8 cover as wide a range of subjects as one could hope for in a journal that believed that 'a bill-head can be as aesthetically pleasing as a bible, that a newspaper can be as typographically arresting as a Nonesuch'. R. S. Hutchings attacks His Majesty's Stationery Office for its failure to follow the recommendations of the 1922 Committee on Type Faces and Government Printing. It is interesting to see that the expenses of the Committee are given as £1,040, of which £908 was spent on experimental work, while the cost of 1,000 copies of the 76-page folio Report, containing many specimen pages and covers and even new designs for the Royal Arms, was £132. Hutchings reaches no conclusions, but suggests either that no one at HMSO was capable of interpreting the Report or that the administration had refused to accept its recommendations. He wonders if the 1922 Report had any greater value than as an addition to typographical *curiosa* and ephemera.

Noel Carrington chose to discuss Victorian street ballads. He laments their passing but resents attempts to revive the Victorian common aesthetic: 'They form part of a popular art which is dead, which should be left to rest in peace and not disinterred to create a passing fashion.' Looking at the illustrations one can only agree with Carrington's diagnosis: 'Written, illustrated and set at competitive speed, there was no time for typographic virtuosity.' A similar failing is pinpointed by Denis Peck in his 'Notes on the Typography of Children's Comics'. Peck condemns the 6 point setting in lines measuring up to forty ems, especially bearing in mind the youthful eyes for which the comics are intended. The well-designed *Mickey Mouse Weekly* was among the first to bear resemblance to comics published today, with plenty of colour and the use of Monotype Rockwell in 10 and 12 point; this represented a great advance in the printing of children's comics. Researches by American Linotype staff showed that optimal legibility for children was attained with 12 on 15 point type (Plantin for example) on white unglazed paper.

Robert Harling's article 'Topographical Typography and/or Typographical Topography' is an introduction to nationwide ephemera, being a discussion of signs and names, on offices, pubs, letter-boxes, notices and milestones. It is worth mentioning here an editorial feature which was used with great effect in issue Nos. 7 and 8: that is the extended caption. Instead of constant reference from text to illustrations, this more efficient method gave discussion of many illustrations in the form of captions of 100 to 200 words, occasionally going further by quoting

49. *Typography* No. 8: 'Victorian Street Ballads' by Noel Carrington.

Victorian Street Ballads:

Notes on a Neglected Popular Art

*Notes on one of the most interesting
facets of Victoriana—for the sociologist,
the historian and the typographer.
The author traces the history of these
ballads and shows an analogy between
the street ballad and the 'penny paper'*

Noel Carrington

VICTORIAN PRINTING, like everything else Victorian, has long been a subject of horror-raised hands or easy jibes, and certainly its defects are numerous, but in some fields it had virtues which are to be admired. In particular I mean its vigour and colour. As printing infallibly reflects the character of any society, so you recognize in the popular, as apart from the genteel, productions of Victorian printers the same racy, forceful temperament of the lower orders that Dickens immortalized – Sam Weller, Mr. Micawber and a whole gallery of types. Dr. John Johnson has fortunately rescued an enormous variety of unconsidered printed sheets from which the student and social historian has more than enough to learn. His museum contains many excellent specimens of English popular art. Perhaps the most beautiful are the lithographed song book covers which reflect the equally popular art of the music hall. The street ballads are on a rather lower plane, though they qualify for a place in any study of the printers' craft.

Some day I hope somebody will make a worthy study of popular art in England. Almost every other phase of our art, all too often of no particular distinction, has been studied. But so little real popular art now remains that a collection of its best representative pieces is long overdue. There can be no question of revival because it is a thing which can only develop at a certain stage of civilization. It cannot coexist with art schools and art criticism. In England it has seldom been of the highest order. We have never had a

peasant art like the Polish or Mexican, nor folk songs nor dances like the Russian or Balinese. Perhaps our civilization has never been sufficiently static.

The street ballads of the nineteenth century, however, bring to a somewhat inglorious close a popular art which reaches back into the dim beginnings of our race and which in its heyday gave us pieces which deservedly rank as great poetry. The decline of the ballad was slow, coinciding with the gradual debasement in status of the labourer and craftsman. Its final demise was deplored even in the fifties of the last century, but I believe that great occasions, such as a royal death, even now produce a broadsheet of popular lament. By the beginning of the nineteenth century the ballad had become debased to a level of crude doggerel verse, and the versifiers were for the most part pothouse moralizers with a gift of the gab. Their most popular subjects were murder and rape. Love affairs with an unfortunate ending had always been the ballad-mongers' stock in trade. Drinking songs could hardly hold their own against the rising tide of earnestness which flavours many a tale. Lastly the street ballad was the underdog's voice of protest against licensing laws, royal extravagance and low wages, all of which crop up with rather tedious regularity. In most respects the subject matter is not dissimilar to that of the modern Sunday paper, except that royalty was treated with less deference. This, for instance, from a ballad entitled *Queen Victoria's Baby* :

> 'About one in the morn, as I heard say,
> The Queen she felt in a curious way.
> She woke her husband, who said with great sorrow,
> "Oh can't you, my love, put it off till to-morrow?
> For I am so sleepy and I don't want a baby."
> "Ah," says she, "but I will have a baby".'

The Prince Consort, it seems evident, was not a popular figure with the masses.

There was naturally a certain amount of bawdiness, but probably less than in earlier centuries. There is the same kind of coarseness that you get to-day in the music hall, and the rewards for virtue seem to be as certain as we are assured they are to-day. Indeed, the music hall songster is the lineal descendant of the ballad-writer, and no doubt also helped to put a nail in his coffin.

The ballads have found collectors from early times, the most famous collection being Percy's *Reliques*, made chiefly from those in oral tradition. Pepys left his large collection, which had been begun by Selden, to Magdalene College. The largest Victorian collection was made by the Rev. S. Baring Gould and is now housed at the British Museum. Ballads have always served the historian in the way that Mass Observation is used to-day. In 1871 there was published *Curiosities of Street Literature* by Charles Hindley, who followed it up with two histories of the Catnach Press. These books, painstaking and discursive, are very valuable

another writer on the same subject. This device is most effective. though surprisingly it does not seem to be employed much nowadays. Harling terms these notes 'the odd and random reflections of a peripatetic typographer'; whatever they are, they make good reading for anyone interested in letter forms as well as providing a new angle on some sociological aspects. They also constitute Harling's last article before war broke out. It is coincidental, but amusing, to notice that this article was rounded off with reference to the typography of ships' names, but 'surely when we find ourselves at sea, this, of all moments, is the time to decide that we have gone far enough with topographical typography and/or typographical topography.' The coincidence arises in the fact that Robert Harling, on the outbreak of war, was to volunteer for service with the Navy, thus bringing *Typography* to an abrupt finish.

Robert Harling's main achievement as editor of *Typography* was to bring a scholarly attitude to bear on modern aspects of print design and technology. Put simplistically, it might be said that *Typography* represented the printer's manual beside the textbook of Simon's *Signature*, the practical against the theoretical. After the war, Harling and Shand again worked together on a journal called *Alphabet and Image*, which adopted the same modern attitude as *Typography*. Once again, Harling's contemporary editorial policy coupled with the immaculate presswork of the Shenval Press was to earn the approbation of bibliophile and businessman alike.

50. *Typography* No. 8:
'Topographical Typography and/or Typographical Topography' by Robert Harling.

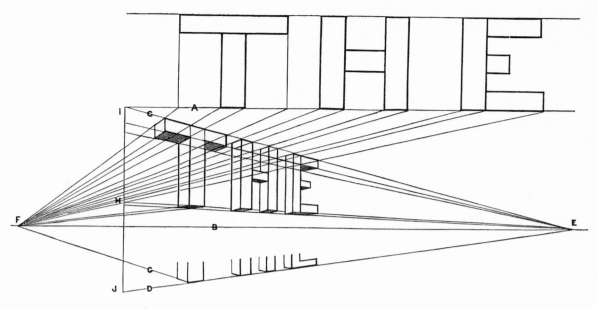

Nineteenth-century theory ↑ and twentieth-century fact →

In the heyday of Victorianism, theories abounded for the budding artist and craftsman. Even the comparatively simple business of signwriting was encumbered with a superfluity of detailed advice. Note, for instance, these explicit particulars from Callingham's MANUAL OF SIGNWRITING *published in 1871, 'illustrating the rules of perspective as they apply to the art of lettering':*

'The student having set out the letters, or elevation, let him make the vertical line I H of the same measurement as the height of the letters in the elevation, and let the horizontal line B be a trifle lower down than the bottom of the vertical line I H. Having drawn the horizontal line B, let E be the vanishing point. From the top of the vertical line at I, draw the oblique line C to the vanishing point E; then from the vertical line I J draw the line H for the bottom of the letters; these two lines represent the perspective inclination of the upper and lower lines of the geometrical drawing or elevation—that is, THE' . . . and so on for another two pages to introduce most of the other alphabetical characters, but space cannot be found for fuller extracts showing how 'to ascertain the correct perspective of the horizontal top of the T', or how the line D shows 'how the letters would recede towards vanishing point if they were of greater depth.'

To-day, as we see on the right, things are somewhat simpler. We have the ready-made alphabets of Gill and Munday to help a nation of shopkeepers towards some degree of clarity in expression and presentation.

street signs (using sometimes a sans serif not unlike Stephenson Blake's Condensed Sans No. 7, and at others the beautifully compact *fraktur* characters); the unfailing taste of the lettering, based on the Condensed *Didot* types, in so many French posters and announcements, and the rather poor lettering in the otherwise highly civilized Sweden. Nations, it seems, do not always get the lettering they deserve.

Journeys nearer home are also made more interesting by this study. I have yet to see more distinguished lettering than that used by the Georgian, Regency and early Victorian sign-writers for their fascias and public notices. Even the dingy present-day Albany Street in north-west London retains one or two reminders of that John Bullish lettering, and Kennington and Hampstead can also show us many interesting survivals. Only now are we beginning to see once again that lettering is an important feature in any urban vista.

Perhaps that is the most disturbing factor which comes out of all these recollections: the singular lack of interest shown by contemporary architects in their consideration of lettering. Strange and extraordinary, for the architect's training is supposed to provide a wider appreciation of æsthetic values than any other curriculum. Yet how often we see a quite well-designed shop ruined by the incredible lettering used on the fascia. Such a sight is a commonplace of urban architecture. Had the architect's training included some elementary work in the virtues of sound lettering, such things could never be.

In recent years some effort has been made to convert architects from this waywardness, and to-day there is no excuse for the designer of any building to mar sound work by unsound lettering. The typographical work of Eric Gill has had a noticeable influence upon this aspect of the work

Conclusion

STANLEY MORISON DEFINED TYPOGRAPHY as 'the craft of rightly disposing printing material in accordance with a specific purpose; of so arranging the letters, distributing the space and controlling the type as to aid to the maximum the reader's comprehension of the text.' Clearly the three journals considered here were concerned with a far wider range of subjects than could be directly related to Morison's specification. Penetrating articles on print management, techniques of illustration, binding and decoration, on minute aspects of the history of printing or the graphic arts, can be variously labelled as book production, bibliography or the criticism of art. But even outside their own fields, the editors' typographic skills are apparent in the design of each journal, each effectively showing 'types at work'. This is why the journals have received worldwide acclaim – they were themselves the best examples of what they advocated.

The typographical periodicals of this period had a further design advantage over literary journals (such as *Blast*, ed. Wyndham Lewis; *The Criterion*, ed. T. S. Eliot; *Life and Letters*, ed. Desmond MacCarthy) – they were produced by the finest printers in this country. Herbert Simon points out that the great success formula of the early issues of *The Fleuron* was 'participation between Oliver Simon typographer and editor and Harold Curwen controller of production relying on the skilled staff of the Plaistow works'.[1] Such understanding was an essential element of the partnerships of Morison and Lewis, and of Harling and Shand.

Two of these partnerships produced further typographical periodicals after 1945. Simon edited *Signature* New Series, eighteen issues appearing between 1946 and 1955, costing the subscriber relatively less than its predecessor. Harling continued *Typography* as *Alphabet and Image*, later abbreviated to *Image*. Morison retained the editorship of the *Times Literary Supplement* from 1945 to 1947; he had long coveted a journalistic job and made many useful changes during the short time he allowed himself. As far as printing was concerned, however, Morison confined himself to monographs.

The quality of production of these interwar journals was excellent. It is a delight to hold and examine them: with their colour, insets, type specimens, and invariably immaculate typesetting, all united by fine design, they eclipse many of the books on which they cast typographical comment. They are the ultimate product of what has been seen as a renaissance in English printing. Yet fifty years ago, *The Fleuron* cost one guinea; ten years later, three issues of *Signature* cost seven shillings and four issues of *Typography* ten shillings. Now, quite rightly, they are collectors' pieces; this came about largely because of their comparative rarity, but also because of the legendary atmosphere that hung about them. I hope that those who have read this book will find my own enthusiasm sufficiently infectious to see the originals for themselves.

Bernard Newdigate wrote in *The Fleuron* No. 1: 'Whether the quality of the work is made better or worse by the invention or development of any ancillary art or method depends on the way in which the art or method is used and applied rather than upon any inherent excellence or defect in the method itself.' If the typographer is possessed of the wisdom contained between the covers of *The Fleuron*, *Signature* and *Typography*, he cannot be better equipped to tackle the enigmatic vagaries of the as yet undesigned book.

Notes

Introduction

1 H. Halliday Sparling, *The Kelmscott Press and William Morris Master-Craftsman* (Dawson, London, 1975), Appendix A (Note by William Morris on his aims in founding the Kelmscott Press).
2 *Ibid.*
3 H. R. Dent (ed.), *The House of Dent 1888–1938* (London, 1938), 'The Memoirs of J. M. Dent', p.125.
4 Notes, *The Imprint* No. 1, 1913.
5 *Ibid.*
6 Leslie Owens, *J. H. Mason 1875–1951 Scholar-Printer* (Frederick Muller, 1976), p.122.

The Fleuron

1 Francis Meynell, *My Lives* (Bodley Head, London, 1971), p.148.
2 Oliver Simon, *Printer and Playground* (Faber & Faber, London, 1956), p.27.
3 James Moran, *Stanley Morison – His Typographical Achievement* (Lund Humphries, London, 1971), p.89.
4 Oliver Simon, *Printer and Playground*, p.31.
5 The prospectus of *The Fleuron*, 1923.
6 Herbert Simon, *Song and Words – A History of the Curwen Press* (Allen & Unwin, London, 1973), p.171.
7 Moran, *Stanley Morison*, p.92.
8 Letter, Morison to Oliver Simon, 1954, in Nicolas Barker, *Stanley Morison* (Macmillan, London, 1972), p.450.
9 Letter, Morison to D. B. Updike, in Barker, *Stanley Morison*, p.134.
10 Herbert Simon, *Song and Words*.
11 Oliver Simon, *Curwen Press Miscellany* (Soncino Press, London, 1931).

12 'Memorandum', Morison to Frederic and Beatrice Warde, 10 July 1925, in Barker, *Stanley Morison*.

13 Stanley Morison, *A Tally of Types*, ed. Brooke Crutchley (Cambridge University Press, 1973), p.80.

14 Letter, Morison to John Holroyd Reece, 10 September 1929, in Barker, *Stanley Morison*.

15 Barker, *Stanley Morison*, p.215.

16 Letter, Morison to Jan van Krimpen, February 1931, in Barker, *Stanley Morison*.

17 Moran, *Stanley Morison*, p.107.

Signature
1 Oliver Simon, *Printer and Playground*, p.128.

2 Herbert Simon, *Song and Words*, p.231.

3 Oliver Simon, *Printer and Playground*, p.134.

4 Editorial Note, *Signature* No. 14, May 1940.

5 Editorial Note, *Signature* No. 15, December 1940.

6 Oliver Simon, *Printer and Playground*, p.135.

7 Editorial Note, *Signature* New Series No. 1, July 1946.

Typography
1 Introductory Note, *Typography* No. 1, November 1936.

2 The prospectus of *Typography*, 1936.

3 Letter, Harling to the author, 13 June 1978.

4 Introductory Note, *Typography* No. 4, Autumn 1937.

5 Letter, Harling to the author, 13 June 1978.

6 Editorial Note, *Typography* No. 6, Summer 1938.

7 Notes, *Typography* No. 7, Winter 1938.

Conclusion
1 Herbert Simon, *Song and Words*, p.171.

Appendix I

THE FLEURON, A Journal of Typography

No. 1 Ed. Oliver Simon, At the Office of The Fleuron, London, 1923, 21s. Demy quarto (11⅛ins. × 8¾ins.), 138pp., Monotype Garamond

Articles
Francis Meynell and Stanley Morison 'Printers' Flowers and Arabesques'
William Rothenstein 'T. J. Cobden-Sanderson'
Holbrook Jackson 'Claud Lovat Fraser'
Percy J. Smith 'Initial Letters in the Printed Book'
Oliver Simon 'The Title Page'
Bernard H. Newdigate 'Respice and Prospice'
D. B. Updike 'The "Lost" Caslon Specimen of 1748'
Herbert Simon 'Notes on Printers' Marks'

Books Reviewed
D. B. Updike, *Printing Types*; HMSO, *Report of the Committee appointed to select the best faces of type and modes of display for Government printing*; F. W. Goudy, *Elements of Lettering*; W. Gamble (ed.), *Penrose's Annual*; Clarendon Press, *Some Account of the Oxford University Press*

No. 2 Ed. Oliver Simon, At the Office of The Fleuron, London, 1924, 21s. Demy quarto (11⅛ins. × 8¾ins.), 119pp., Monotype Baskerville

Articles
Julius Meier-Graefe 'Emil Rudolf Weiss'
D. B. Updike 'On the Planning of Printing'

Pierre Gusman 'Edouard Pelletan'
Stanley Morison 'Towards an Ideal Type'
Bernard H. Newdigate 'Mr C. H. St John Hornby's Ashendene Press'
Holbrook Jackson 'The Nonage of Nineteenth-Century Printing in England'
Roger Ingpen 'Decorated Papers'

Books Reviewed
S. Morison, *On Type Faces*; F. Meynell (attr.) *Typography*; N. J. Hussung, *Buch und Buchbeinband*; C. Saunier, *Les Décorateurs du Livre*; M. Salaman, *British Book Illustration*; W. Gamble, *Music Engraving and Printing*

No. 3 Ed. Oliver Simon, At the Office of The Fleuron, London, 1924, 21s. Demy quarto (11⅛ins. × 8¾ins.), 135pp., Monotype Caslon

Articles
W. A. Dwiggins 'D. B. Updike and the Merrymount Press'
Randolph Schwabe 'Albert Rutherston' (bibliography by T. Balston)
A. F. Johnson and Stanley Morison 'The Chancery Types of Italy and France'
Harold Child 'The Amateur and Printing'
P. J. Angoulvent 'The Development of the Book'
Frank Sidgwick 'Contemporary Printers I – Stanley Morison'
Method Kalab 'Czechoslovak Printing'
Hubert Foss 'Modern Styles in Music Printing'

Books Reviewed
S. Morison, *Four Centuries of Fine Printing*; G. Keynes, *William Pickering Publisher*; H. R. Plomer, *English Printers' Ornaments*; H. Jackson (introd.) *Catalogue Raisonné of Books Printed at the Curwen Press*

No. 4 Ed. Oliver Simon, At the Office of The Fleuron, London, 1925, 21s. Demy quarto (11⅛ins. × 8¾ins.), 164pp., Monotype Caslon

Articles
Stanley Morison 'On Script Types'
Holbrook Jackson 'Robert Bridges, George Moore, Bernard Shaw and Printing'
Frank Sidgwick 'The Typographical Work of Percy Smith'
Bernard H. Newdigate 'Contemporary Printers II – Emery Walker'
Hanna Kiel 'Tendencies in German Book-Printing Since 1914'
Frederic Warde 'On the Work of Bruce Rogers'

Books Reviewed
S. Morison, *Modern Fine Printing*; D. B. Updike, *In the Day's Work*; H. Halliday Sparling, *The Kelmscott Press and William Morris Master-Craftsman*

No. 5 Ed. Stanley Morison, Cambridge University Press/Doubleday Doran, 1926, 21s. Demy quarto (11⅛ins. × 8¾ins.), 205pp., Monotype Barbou

Articles
Julius Rodenberg 'The Work of Karl Klingspor'
Paul Istel 'J. R. Laboureur Illustrator' (translated by X. M. Boulestin)
H. V. Marrot 'William Bulmer'
Stanley Morison 'Towards an Ideal Type'
Paul Beaujon 'The "Garamond" Types'

Books Reviewed
P. Jessen, *Meister der Schreibkunst*; H. R. Plomer, *Wynkyn de Worde and His Contemporaries*; F. Warde, *Bruce Rogers Designer of Books*

No. 6 Ed. Stanley Morison, Cambridge University Press/Doubleday Doran, 1928, 21s. Demy quarto (11⅛ins. × 8¾ins.), 234pp., Monotype Barbou

Articles
Robert Windisch 'The Work of Rudolf Koch'
A. F. Johnson 'Geofroy Tory'
Paul Beaujon 'On Decorative Printing in America'
Stanley Morison 'Decorative Types'
Luc Benoist 'Bernard Naudin, Illustrator'
D. B. Updike (ed.) 'Types of Gille *fils*'

Book Reviewed
J. Rodenberg, *Die Deutsche Schriftgiesserei*

Types Reviewed
Lutetia Italic (J. van Krimpen, Enschedé); Romain (E. R. Weiss, Bauer); Baskerville (Stempel); Pastonchi (F. Pastonchi, Monotype); New Hellenic (V. Scholderer, Monotype); Meidoorn (S. H. de Roos, privately cut)

No. 7 Ed. Stanley Morison, Cambridge University Press/Doubleday Doran, 1930, 21s. Demy quarto (11⅛ins. × 8¾ins.), 246pp., Monotype Barbou, with Postscript to *The Fleuron* by Stanley Morison and Index to *The Fleuron* compiled by A. F. Johnson

Articles
Jan van Krimpen 'Typography in Holland'
Paul Beaujon 'Eric Gill Sculptor of Letters'
Stanley Morison 'First Principles of Typography'
Rudolf Koch 'Heinrich Holz'
A. J. A. Symons 'An Unacknowledged Movement in Fine Printing'
Friedrich Ewald 'The Officina Bodoni'
D. B. Updike 'Thomas Maitland Cleland'
A. F. Johnson, Paul Beaujon, Graham Pollard and Stanley Morison 'Footnotes to Book Production' (short articles)

Books Reviewed
V. Scholderer, *Greek Printing Types 1465–1927*; S. Morison, *Incunabula in the British Museum*; W. D. Orcutt, *The Book in Italy during the 15th and 16th Centuries Shown in Facsimile Reproductions*

Types Reviewed
Centaur Roman (B. Rogers, Monotype); Bembo (Monotype); Treyford (G. Hewitt); Antigone Greek (J. van Krimpen, Enschedé); Bernhard (L. Bernhard, Bauer); Goudy Modern (F. W. Goudy, Monotype); Romanée (J. van Krimpen, Enschedé); Perpetua (E. Gill, Monotype)

SIGNATURE, A Quadrimestrial of Typography and the Graphic Arts

No. 1 Ed. Oliver Simon, Museum St, London, November 1935, 3s. 9¾ins. × 7⅜ins., 62pp., Monotype Walbaum (collotypes printed by the Chiswick Press)

Articles
Holbrook Jackson 'A Sanctuary of Printing'
Paul Nash 'New Draughtsmen'
Oliver Simon 'The Printed and Published Wood-Engravings of Eric Ravilious'
Oliver Simon 'Initial Letters by Barnett Freedman'

Books Reviewed
W. Turner Berry and A. F. Johnson, *Catalogue of Specimens of Printing Types by English and Scottish Printers and Founders 1665–1830*; C. H. St John Hornby, *A Descriptive Bibliography of the Books Printed at the Ashendene Press 1895–1935*

No. 2 Ed. Oliver Simon, Museum St, London, March 1936, 3s. 9¾ins. × 7⅜ins., 52pp., Monotype Walbaum

Articles
Barnett Freedman 'Lithography: A Printer's Paradise'
James Laver 'Two Drawings'
John Carter 'The Woodcut Calligraphy of Reynolds Stone'
Desmond Flower 'Modern English Handwriting'
Frank Sidgwick 'The Double Crown Club'
Harry Carter 'The New Tauchnitz Format'

Book Reviewed
F. Isaac, *English Printers' Types of the 16th Century*

No. 3 Ed. Oliver Simon, Museum St, London, July 1936, 3s. 9¾ins. × 7⅜ins., 52pp., Monotype Walbaum

Articles
Stanley Morison 'On Advertisement Settings'
Graham Sutherland 'A Trend in English Draughtsmanship'
A. F. Johnson 'English Typography in the Seventeenth Century'
Hamish Miles 'The Printed Work of Edward Bawden'

Books Reviewed
M. Audin, *Les Livres Typographiques des Fonderies Françaises créés avant 1800*; S. Morison, *First Principles of Typography*; A. J. A. Symons, F. Meynell and D. Flower, *The Nonesuch Century*; R. B. Fishenden (ed.) *Penrose's Annual*; J. Tschichold, *Typographische Gestaltung*

Type Reviewed
Albertus Titling (B. Wolpe, Monotype)

No. 4 Ed. Oliver Simon, Great Russell St, London, November 1936, 3s. 9¾ins. × 7⅜ins., 55pp., Monotype Walbaum

Articles
Paul Beaujon 'Progress in Bible Production'
Kenneth Clark 'A Note on Three Illustrations to *Wuthering Heights*'
Desmond Flower 'A Brief Survey of English Handwriting 1500–1936'

A. F. Johnson, Enid Marks and Christian Barman 'The Typographic Studies of Stanley Morison'

Type Reviewed
'Collins' Fontana (Monotype) advised by G. Mardersteig

No. 5 Ed. Oliver Simon, Great Russell St, London, March 1937, 3s. 9¾ins. × 7⅜ins., 54pp., Monotype Walbaum

Articles
Paul Nash 'Surrealism and the Illustrated Book'
Ellic Howe 'An Introduction to Hebrew Typography'
Oliver Simon 'The Printed Work of Barnett Freedman'
Vivian Ridler 'Desiderata for the Sanctuary of Printing'
John Piper 'Lithography by Eric Ravilious of Shop Fronts'

Books Reviewed
E. Gill, *An Essay on Typography*; P. J. Smith, *Lettering: A Handbook of Modern Alphabets*; *Cesky Bibliofil* No. 8

No. 6 Ed. Oliver Simon, Great Russell St, London, July 1937, 3s. 9¾ins. × 7⅜ins., 54pp., Monotype Walbaum

Articles
John Piper 'Invention in Colour' (drawing)
Desmond Flower 'Firmin Didot and His Family'
H. S. Williamson 'They Marched with Banners'
Graham Sutherland 'Graven Images: Line Engraving and the Illustrated Book'
J. E. Pouterman 'René Ben Sussan'
Harry Carter 'Monotype van Dijck and Christoffel van Dijck'

Books Reviewed
M. Wheeler (ed.) *Modern Painters and Sculptors as Illustrators*; C. P. Rollins (introd.) *The Specimen Books of Binny and Ronaldson 1809–1812*

No. 7 Ed. Oliver Simon, Great Russell St, London, November 1937, 3s. 9¾ins. × 7⅜ins., 52pp., Monotype Walbaum

Articles
Geoffrey Grigson 'Samuel Palmer at Shoreham'
Paul Beaujon 'Some Recent Editions of Shakespeare's Works'
John Piper 'Aspects of Modern Drawing'
Francis Meynell 'Typographic Flowers'

No. 8 Ed. Oliver Simon, Great Russell St, London, March 1938, 3s. 9¾ins. × 7⅜ins., 55pp., Monotype Walbaum

Articles
Ellic Howe 'The Le Bé Family'
Lynton Lamb 'Ambroise Vollard as a Publisher' (bibliography by J. E. Pouterman)
Paul Standard 'The Ampersand – Sign of Continuity'

Book Reviewed
D. B. Updike, *Printing Types* (2nd ed.)

Types Reviewed
Temple Script (Monotype); Sachsenwald Gothic (Monotype)

No. 9 Ed. Oliver Simon, Great Russell St, London, July 1938, 3s. 9¾ins. × 7⅜ins., 54pp., Monotype Walbaum

Articles
Graham Sutherland 'Clegyr-Bria: Etching and Aquatint'
James Wardrop 'Mr Whatman Papermaker'
Desmond Flower 'A Survey of Modern Binding'
Paul Nash 'Openings'
Peggy Laing 'Swelled Rules and Typographic Flourishes'

Book Reviewed
G. Hewitt, *Handwriting: Everyman's Craft*

No. 10 Ed. Oliver Simon, Great Russell St, London, November 1938, 3s. 9¾ins. × 7⅜ins., 56pp., Monotype Walbaum

Articles
John Piper 'Henry Fuseli RA 1741–1825'

Dr Charles Enschedé 'The Elzevier Press and Its Relationship with the Luther Typefoundry'
J. E. Pouterman 'The Publications of Etablissements Nicolas, Wine Merchants, Paris'

Books Reviewed
S. Morison, *The Art of Printing*; H. Jackson, *The Printing of Books*; N. Gray, *Nineteenth-Century Ornamented Types*; B. H. Newdigate, *The Art of the Book*

No. 11 Ed. Oliver Simon, Great Russell St, London, March 1939, 3s. 9¾ins. × 7⅜ins., 55pp., Monotype Walbaum

Articles
Edward Ardizzone 'Evening in Maida Vale' (drawing)
Stanley Morison 'Leipzig as a Centre of Typefoundry'
Olga and Ellic Howe 'Vignettes in Typefounders' Specimen Books'
Holbrook Jackson 'Typographia'
Peggy Laing 'An Aspect of Nineteenth-Century French Jobbing'

No. 12 Ed. Oliver Simon, Great Russell St, London, July 1939, 3s. 9¾ins. × 7⅜ins. 56pp., Monotype Walbaum

Articles
Frances Macdonald 'Stanley Morison' (illustration)
Herbert Read 'Hors de Commerce'
Philip James 'The Pelican Press 1916–1923'
James Wardrop 'Arrighi Revived'
H. P. R. Finberg 'The Hirsch Collection of Decorated Papers'

Books Reviewed
G. W. Ovink, *Legibility, Atmosphere-Value and Forms of Printing Types*; Monotype Corporation, *Leaves out of Books*

No. 13 Ed. Oliver Simon, Great Russell St, London, January 1940, 3s. 9¾ins. × 7⅜ins., 42 pp., Monotype Walbaum

Articles
Paul Beaujon 'The Anthology of Verse as a Typographic Problem'

Geoffrey Grigson 'George Stubbs 1724–1806'
John Betjeman 'Cheltenham'
A. F. Johnson 'Mr van Krimpen's "Romulus"'

Books Reviewed
M. Audin, *Alfred Cartier*; F. Isaac, *An Index to the Early Printed Books in the British Museum*; J. Laver, *A Book of Fanfare Ornaments*

No. 14 Ed. Oliver Simon, North Street, Plaistow, London, May 1940, 3s. 9¾ins. × 7⅜ins., 37pp., Monotype Walbaum

Articles
S. H. Steinberg 'Gutenberg's Germany: Its Economic and Cultural Conditions'
J. E. Pouterman 'Books Illustrated by Pablo Picasso'
J. M. Richards 'Edward Ardizzone'

Books Reviewed
H. J. Keefe, *A Century in Print: The Story of Hazell's 1839–1939*; A. Ruppel, *Johannes Gutenberg: Sein Leben und Sein Werk*; D. B. Updike (introd.), *Bruce Rogers: Jack of All Trades: Master of One*; R. B. Fishenden (ed.), *Penrose's Annual*

No. 15, Ed. Oliver Simon, North St, Plaistow, London, December 1940, 3s. 9¾ins. × 7⅜ins., 36pp., Monotype Walbaum, with Index to *Signature* Nos. 1 to 15

Articles
Stanley Morison 'Anton Janson Identified'
Desmond Flower 'Napoleon's Books'
Nicolete Gray 'Berthold Wolpe'

Books Reviewed
R. Nash and S. Morison, *Calligraphy and Printing in the 16th Century*; P. Hofer, *A Specimen of Fell Type*; Cambridge University Press, *Catalogue: An Exhibition of Printing at the Fitzwilliam Museum*

TYPOGRAPHY

No. 1 Ed. Robert Harling, at the Shenval Press, London, November 1936, 2s. 11ins. × 9ins., 46pp.

Articles
Francis Meynell 'Voices and Vices' (Monotype Plantin)
René Hague 'Reason and Typography' (Monotype Perpetua)
Ellic Howe 'Prologue and Epilogue to Updike' (Monotype Imprint)
James Shand 'The Alphabet and the Printing Press' (Monotype Plantin)
Robert Harling 'Somebody Discovers the Case' (Monotype Plantin)
S. L. Righyni 'News into Type' (Monotype Times New Roman)
Philip James 'Modern Commercial Typography' (Monotype Plantin)
Bernard Griffin 'Kardomah Tea Labels' (Monotype Times New Roman)

Books Reviewed
S. Morison, *First Principles of Typography*; E. Gill, *An Essay on Typography*

Types Reviewed
Beton Medium Condensed (H. Jost, Bauer); Kayo (E. Gill, Monotype); Sketch
(Ludwig and Mayer)

No. 2 Ed. Robert Harling, at the Shenval Press, London, Spring 1937, 2s. 11ins ×
9ins., 48pp.

Articles
John Betjeman 'Shell Guide to Typography' (Monotype Modern)
Ellic Howe 'Typefounding and Typesetting' (Monotype Imprint)
John Rayner 'Features for Two Millions' (Monotype Plantin)
Anthony W. Bell 'The Honour of Your Company' (Monotype Baskerville)
James Shand 'Slug' (Linotype Baskerville)
J. C. Allsop 'Tram Ticket Typography' (Monotype Plantin)
Molly Fordham 'The Work of Feliks Topolski' (Monotype Garamond)

Types Reviewed
Allegro (Ludwig and Mayer); Cartoon Bold and Light (Bauer); Tempest Titling
(B. Wolpe, Fanfare Press); Marina Script (Stephenson Blake); Thorne Shaded (R.
Thorne, Stephenson Blake)

No. 3 Ed. Robert Harling, at the Shenval Press, London, Summer 1937, 2s. 11ins. ×
9ins., 54pp.

Articles
Jan Tschichold 'Type Mixtures' (Monotype Bodoni)
Herbert Read 'The Work of Ashley Havinden' (Monotype Bodoni)

Frederick W. Goudy 'Ands and Ampersands'
Ellic Howe 'From Bewick to the Half-Tone Process'
Howard Wadman 'Left-Wing Layout'
Peggy Laing 'Interpretative Typography Applied to School Geometry'
Allen Hutt 'The Front Page'

Books Reviewed
E. Allen, *Newspaper Makeup*; Mergenthaler Linotype Corporation, *Peter Piper's Practical Principles of Plain and Perfect Pronunciation*

Types Reviewed
Egmont (S. H. de Roos, Intertype); Slimblack (Deberny et Peignot); City (G. Trump, Berthold); Offenbach Light and Medium (R. Koch, Klingspor); Falstaff (Monotype)

No. 4 Ed. Robert Harling, at the Shenval Press, London, Autumn 1937, 2s. 11ins. × 9ins., 44pp.

Articles
Harry Carter 'The Optical Scale in Typefounding' (Monotype Times Roman)
Misha Black 'The Dust Wrapper' (Monotype Plantin)
Gordon Bromley 'The Work of Edmond Kapp' (Monotype Walbaum)
Roland Knaster 'The Paper-Valentine' (Monotype Walbaum)
Alfred Fairbank 'Handwriting Reform' (Monotype Narrow Bembo)
James Shand 'American Visit' (Monotype Plantin)

Books Reviewed
J. L. Martin, B. Nicholson and N. Gabo (ed.), *Circle*; Nonesuch Press, *Nonesuch Dickensiana*

Types Reviewed
Perpetua Light Titling (Monotype); Temple Script (Monotype); Claudius (R. Koch, Klingspor); Ludlow Hauser Script (G. Hauser, Ludlow); Scarab (Stephenson Blake); Bessemer (D. Megaw, Stevens Shanks)

No. 5 Ed. Robert Harling, at the Shenval Press, London, Spring 1938, 2s. 11ins. × 9ins., 58pp.

Articles

Eric Gill 'The Work of Denis Tegetmeier' (handset Bunyan)

S. L. Righyni 'The Morning Post' (Monotype Plantin)

Christian Barman 'Timetable Typography' (Monotype Plantin)

Konrad Bauer 'The Bauer Typefoundry' (Bauer Bodoni)

Harry Carter 'Updike's Printing Types' (Monotype Plantin)

John Gloag 'A Paul Nash Portfolio' (Monotype Plantin)

Howard Wadman 'The English Print' (Monotype Plantin)

Denis Butlin 'Patent Medicine Advertising' (Monotype Plantin)

John E. Allen 'Modern Newspaper Make-Up' (Linotype Excelsior)

Types Reviewed

Peignot (A. M. Cassandre, Deberny et Peignot); Legend (F. H. E. Schneider, Bauer); Gill Medium Condensed and Gill Bold Extra Condensed (E. Gill, Monotype); Coronation (Stephenson Blake); Times Roman Wide (Monotype)

No. 6 Ed. Robert Harling, at the Shenval Press, London, Summer 1938, 2s. 11ins. × 9ins., 58pp.

Articles

S. L. Righyni 'The Typography of the Provincial Press' (Monotype Times Roman)

Imre Reiner 'An Autobiographical Fragment' (Monotype Walbaum)

A. F. Johnson 'Notes on Some Seventeenth-Century English Types' (Monotype Imprint)

John Betjeman 'Ecclesiastical Typography' (Monotype Plantin)

'From Cover to Cover' (Monotype Bodoni)

Books Reviewed

C. Yee, *Chinese Calligraphy; An Introduction to its Aesthetic and Technique*; G. Hewitt, *Handwriting: Everyman's Craft*; Bauer Typefoundry, *Birth and Growth of a German Type-Foundry: To Commemorate the Centenary of the Establishment of the Bauer Type-Foundry*; A. R. Hopper, *Hopper's Type Tables*; W. Klinefelter, *A Bibliographical Check-List of Christmas Books*

Types Reviewed

Floride (I. Reiner, Deberny et Peignot); Elizabeth (Bauer); Ludlow Coronet Script (Ludlow); Dorchester Script (Monotype); Grosvenor Script (Monotype)

No. 7 Ed. Robert Harling, at the Shenval Press, London, Winter 1938, 2s. 11ins. ×
9 ins., 60pp., Monotype Times Roman

Articles
Holbrook Jackson 'The Dictatorship of the Lay-Out Man'
Ashley Havinden 'Visual Expression'
Roland Knaster 'Early Children's ABC's'
James Shand 'Five Books about Books'
Denis Megaw 'Twentieth-Century Sans Serif Types'
John Carter 'The Typography of the Cheap Reprint Series'

Books Reviewed
N. Gray, *Nineteenth-Century Types*; W. Steed, *The Press*

Types Reviewed
Post-Roman (Berthold); Playbill (R. Harling, Stephenson Blake); Matura (Mono-
type); Lilith (Bauer); Lydian and Lydian Italic (W. Chappell, American Type
Founders); Gladiola (Stempel)

No. 8 Ed. Robert Harling, at the Shenval Press, London, Summer 1939, 2s. 11ins. ×
9ins., 58pp., Monotype Plantin

Articles
R. S. Hutchings 'Lament for a Bluebook Bureaucracy'
Noel Carrington 'Victorian Street Ballads'
Denis Peck 'The Typography of Children's Comics'
Robert Harling 'Topographical Typography and/or Typographical Topography'
Edith Olivier 'Rex Whistler's Book Decorations'

Books Reviewed
L. Moholy-Nagy, *The New Vision*; R. J. Beedham, *Wood Engraving*

Types Reviewed
Amanda Script (Stephenson Blake); Caprice (Berthold); Corvinus Skyline (I.
Reiner, Bauer); Slender and Slender Bold (Ludwig and Mayer); Chisel (R. Harling,
Stephenson Blake); Tea Chest (R. Harling, Stephenson Blake)

Appendix II

Harold Curwen
Grandson of John Curwen, the founder of the Curwen Press, Harold Curwen studied calligraphy under Edward Johnston at the Central School of Arts and Crafts. He was a founder member of the Design and Industries Association in 1916 and in 1918 he appointed Joseph Thorp as design consultant to the Press. Together they advocated the 'Spirit of Joy in Printing', often using the brightly coloured work of Claud Lovat Fraser, the first of the many artists who were to work at Curwen. He and Oliver Simon were responsible for the brilliant period of innovation which transformed the Curwen Press from a small music printer to an eminent colour printing house respected throughout the world. He died in 1949.

Robert Harling
Robert Harling was appointed art director of a leading advertising agency in his twenties and became deeply interested in display typography, designing Playbill, Chisel, Tea Chest, Keyboard and other types for Stephenson Blake, the Sheffield typefounders. He started *Typography* with James Shand and Ellic Howe in 1936. After the war, in which he served in the RNVR, he and Shand began to publish *Alphabet and Image* (later *Image*). For several years he has edited *House & Garden*. He is typographical adviser to *The Sunday Times*, which provided authentic background material for *The Paper Palace* and his other newspaper novels.

Ellic Howe
Ellic Howe, with Robert Harling, was the youngest of those involved in the subject of this volume. After Oxford, he became deeply interested in historical and technical aspects of typography. Friendship with Shand involved him in the early stages of the production of *Typography*, but he later concentrated on typographical research in the USA, Germany and France, and the assembly of a remarkable typographical library. He greatly aided Stanley Morison in his researches during the later years of that eminent scholar's life.

Walter Lewis

Walter Lewis worked for Ballantyne & Co. from 1903 to 1916. In 1919 he met Charles Hobson, an advertising agent. They decided to form a printing company together; Lewis spent a year planning a layout of the factory and purchasing the equipment. The Cloister Press was started in 1921 with Stanley Morison as typographical adviser. Lewis left the Press in 1922 and was soon recommended to replace J. B. Peace, the University Printer at Cambridge; on his appointment in 1923 he immediately began to pursue the typographical suggestions of Bruce Rogers, supported by Morison, who became typographical adviser there in 1925. Lewis remained in this post until he retired in 1944. He died in 1960.

Stanley Morison

In 1913, Stanley Morison applied to Gerard Meynell for his first job in typography, assisting with the publication of *The Imprint*. During the First World War, he worked with Francis Meynell at Burns & Oates; later he was imprisoned as a conscientious objector. At the end of the war, Morison joined the Pelican Press, and published his first book, *The Craft of Printing: Notes on the History of Type Forms*, in 1921. He then acted as typographical adviser to the short-lived Cloister Press. He became adviser on typographic design to the Monotype Corporation in 1923, and to Cambridge University Press in 1925. In 1931, the redesigned *The Times* appeared, incorporating Morison's Times New Roman typeface. His legacy of books, pamphlets and articles is remarkable both for its quantity and for its quality. Three handlists of his work have been compiled, by Ellic Howe, John Carter and Graham Pollard, and P. M. Handover. Stanley Morison died in 1967.

James Shand

James Shand, son of the printer Alexander Shand, studied at the London School of Printing from 1923 to 1925, emerging with the City and Guilds Full Technological Certificate. He was appointed Assistant Printer under Dr John Johnson at Oxford University Press in 1929. He left in 1930 and founded the Shenval Press imprint, whose work was executed by Gee & Co., of which his father was a director. In 1931, the family acquired Simson & Co. in Hertford and James Shand became its managing director. The firm later became Simson Shand Ltd. His work with Robert Harling continued after the war with *Alphabet and Image* and the Art and Technics imprint. He was president of the Double Crown Club in 1947. He died in 1967.

Oliver Simon

In 1919, after a brief period with the old lithographic and collotype firm Charles Whittington & Griggs, Oliver Simon joined the Curwen Press, of which he eventually became chairman. After a 'probationary' year, he was appointed to sell print to book publishers. To set an example, he established a small publishing enterprise, the Office of The Fleuron, later to be absorbed by the Soncino Press in 1929. He is best remembered for his success in using the work of many of the great artists of the time to illustrate Curwen books. His classic *Introduction to Typography* was published in 1945, and his autobiography *Printer and Playground* in 1956. He died in 1956.

Beatrice Warde

Born in New York, Beatrice Becker was appointed assistant to H. L. Bullen, Librarian of the American Type Founders Library in Jersey City. She married Frederic Warde, Printer to Princeton University. They travelled to England in 1925; as 'Paul Beaujon' she soon established her reputation with 'The "Garamond" Types' published in *The Fleuron* No. 5. She was invited to edit the *Monotype Recorder* and subsequently became publicity manager for the Monotype Corporation. She died in 1969.

Select Bibliography

Barker, N. *Stanley Morison*, Macmillan, London, 1972.

Crutchley, B. *Two Men: Walter Lewis and Stanley Morison at Cambridge*, privately printed, Cambridge, 1968.

Drinkwater, D. and Rutherston, A. *Claud Lovat Fraser*, Heinemann, London, 1923.

Gill, E. *An Essay on Typography*, Sheed & Ward, London, 1931; 2nd ed. 1936.

Gilmour, P. *Artists at Curwen*, Tate Gallery Publications Department, London, 1977.

Harley, B. *The Curwen Press: A Short History*, privately printed, London, 1970.

Harling, R. *Edward Bawden*, Art & Technics, London, 1950.

Harling, R. *Notes on the Wood-Engravings of Eric Ravilious*, Art & Technics, London, 1946.

Jackson, H. *The Eighteen-Nineties*, Cassell, London, 1913.

Jackson, H. *The Printing of Books*, Cassell, London, 1938.

Johnson, A. F. *Decorative Initial Letters*, Cresset Press, London, 1931.

McLean, R. *Modern Book Design from William Morris to the Present Day*, Faber & Faber, London, 1958.

McLean, R. *Jan Tschichold: Typographer*, Lund Humphries, London, 1975.

Meynell, F. *My Lives*, Bodley Head, London, 1971.

Moran, J. *Stanley Morison: His Typographic Achievement*, Lund Humphries, London, 1971.

Morison, S. *The Art of Printing*, Oxford University Press, London, 1938.

Morison, S. *The Craft of Printing*, Pelican Press, London, 1921.

Morison, S. *First Principles of Typography*, Cambridge University Press, Cambridge, 1930.

Morison, S. *Four Centuries of Fine Printing*, Ernest Benn, London, 1924.

Morison, S. *The History of The Times*, The Times, London, 1935–52.

Morison, S. *John Fell: The University Press and the 'Fell' Types*, Oxford University Press, London, 1967.

Morison, S. *A Tally of Types*, Cambridge University Press, Cambridge, 1953; 2nd ed. 1973.

Myers, R. *The British Book Trade*, André Deutsch, London, 1973.

Nash, P. *A Specimen Book of Pattern Papers Designed for and in Use at the Curwen Press*, The Fleuron, London, 1928.

Newdigate, B. H. *The Art of the Book*, The Studio, London, 1938.

Simon, H. *Song and Words: A History of the Curwen Press*, Allen & Unwin, London, 1973.

Simon, O. *Catalogue Raisonné of Books Printed at the Curwen Press 1920–1923*, Curwen Press, London, 1933.

Simon, O. *Introduction to Typography*, Faber & Faber, London, 1945; 2nd ed. (revised by D. Bland) 1963.

Index

INDEX

This is copy number *43*